MARTIN SWALES

The German Bildungsroman from Wieland to Hesse

PRINCETON UNIVERSITY PRESS
Princeton, N.J.

Copyright © 1978 by Princeton University Press
Published by Princeton University Press,
Princeton, New Jersey
In the United Kingdom: Princeton University Press,
Guildford, Surrey

All Rights Reserved

Library of Congress Cataloging in Publication Data will
be found on the last printed page of this book
Publication of this book has been aided by
a grant from The Andrew W. Mellon Foundation

This book has been composed in VIP Palatino

Printed in the United States of America
by Princeton University Press, Princeton, New Jersey

For
Barker Fairley

Contents

Preface

By any standards, the German Bildungsroman is not an easily accessible novel tradition for the Anglo-Saxon reader. In the concluding chapter of his study *The German Novel* Roy Pascal summarizes both cogently and sympathetically the salient features of this novel genre: its tentative relationship to practicalities, the lack of plasticity in its treatment of personal development, its obstinate tendency toward narrative discursiveness. All this sounds very forbidding—as, indeed, is the length of most actual Bildungsroman texts. In view of these obstacles in particular, I have endeavored to keep this study short and (I hope) approachable. The novels themselves are, of course, highly complex texts, and in my analyses much has been omitted. On the other hand, I have tried to illuminate the structuring principle which, in my view, is at the heart of the genre, and to suggest something of the overall import which the specific works generate. I hope specialist readers will forgive me if certain detailed aspects of the texts receive somewhat cursory consideration.

I would add finally that throughout my work on these novels I have been insistently aware of the foreignness of the Bildungsroman tradition to me as an English novel reader. I believe that this foreignness has supplied creative provocation for my study: I have been concerned to stress the need for a greater awareness in the English-speaking world of this specifically (but not narrowly) German contribution to the European novel tradition. I have been particularly conscious of this need because of both the difficulty and the enrichment that have attended upon my own discovery of the Bildungsroman.

In conclusion, I should like to thank those people who have helped me by discussing many of the issues involved in this study. I think particularly of my wife Erika, of Roy Pascal, of Modris Eksteins, and of the many members of the May 1976 Amherst Colloquium on German Literature who were kind enough to give me the benefit of their reactions to my paper on the Bildungsroman. I am also grateful to my students at London University for the patience, skepticism, and interest with which they greeted my various attempts to lecture on the Bildungsroman.

I owe a particular debt of gratitude to Barker Fairley, who during the academic year 1975-1976 (which I spent in Toronto) gave me consistently the benefit of his superb critical instinct, of his incisive enthusiasm for German and English literature, and, above all, of his friendship. To him I dedicate this study.

Translations throughout, unless otherwise indicated, are my own. I am grateful to the editors of the *Publications of the English Goethe Society*, and to the editors and publishers (J. B. Metzler, Stuttgart) of the *Deutsche Vierteljahrsschrift für Literaturwissenschaft und Geistesgeschichte* for allowing me to draw on material which first appeared in the pages of their journals. My thanks are due to Doris Lessing, to Jonathan Cape Ltd., and to John Cushman Associates Inc. for allowing me to quote the passages from Doris Lessing's *The Summer before the Dark* which figure in the excursus.

Finally, I wish to express my profound gratitude to Princeton University Press for agreeing once again to publish my work, and to their advisers, whose comments and criticisms have helped me more than I can say. R. Miriam Brokaw, Associate Director and Editor at Princeton University Press, has brought her customary blend of kindness, patience, and good sense to bear on the whole process of converting a somewhat chaotic

typescript into manageable form. To her, to all her col-
leagues, and especially to Gretchen Oberfranc, my
exemplary copyeditor, I should like to extend my
warmest thanks.

Martin Swales
May 1977

The German Bildungsroman
from Wieland to Hesse

The highest form of the novel was the novel of personal devel-
opment: a man passed through the richness of the phenomenal
world and attempted to discover its meaning. The idea was
good, but the distribution of forces was wrongly perceived: the
circumstances, the conditions of the world were taken as giv-
en, as overwhelmingly real, the wanderer through them was
weak, humble, obedient. Put more clearly one could say that
the novels were dualistic in structure: on the one hand, an a
priori *moral, theological meaning in the phenomena—and on*
the other, the quester after meaning. If he was a nuisance and
knew of a multiplicity and simultaneity of viewpoints, he was
left with no alternative but to take up the linearity
[Nacheinander] of experience, and in the process it constantly
happened that he would declare the last viewpoint to be the
true one. Abandoning the struggle in resignation or harmony,
he would make his peace, the novel was over, nothing had been
said, simultaneity had not been expressed.

Otto Flake
(1913)

Introduction

Critical literature on the Bildungsroman has for many years[1] followed in the wake of Wilhelm Dilthey's famous definition, derived from his analysis of Goethe's *Wilhelm Meister's Apprenticeship* and of Friedrich Hölderlin's *Hyperion*: "A regulated development within the life of the individual is observed, each of its stages has its own intrinsic value and is at the same time the basis for a higher stage. The dissonances and conflicts of life appear as the necessary growth points through which the individual must pass on his way to maturity and harmony."[2] Dilthey's definition is essentially concerned with the subject matter of the Bildungsroman, and this in itself supplies a certain limitation. No mention is made of how such a thematic statement is generated. Moreover, it seems debatable, to say the least, whether even *Wilhelm Meister's Apprenticeship* depicts that fulfillment and harmony which Dilthey sees as the necessary goal of the Bildungsroman. Yet, in spite of its problematic aspects, Dilthey's *aperçu* has acquired almost canonical status within German literary history.

Given the limitation of this genre definition, it is hardly surprising that there have been a number of iconoclastic voices raised, voices which proclaim that the notion of the Bildungsroman is little better than a pedantic fiction coined by overzealous academics.[3] Such summary dismantling is, of course, very appealing. But it tends to ride roughshod over the whole theoretical

[1] For a summary of the relevant secondary literature see Lothar Köhn, *Entwicklungs- und Bildungsroman* (Stuttgart, 1969).

[2] *Das Erlebnis und die Dichtung* (Leipzig and Bern, 1913), 394.

[3] See for example W. Pabst's onslaught in his article, "Literatur zur Theorie des Romans," *Deutsche Vierteljahrsschrift für Literaturwissenschaft und Geistesgeschichte*, 34 (1960), 264ff. (hereafter cited as *DVLG*).

question of the nature—and definability—of literary genres. The reaction against the "Dilthey school" has led to a jettisoning of the baby with the bathwater.

Of late, a number of innovative attempts to deal with the Bildungsroman have been made, attempts which emphasize structural and narrative (rather than thematic) features. Despite their many differences, the recent studies by Jürgen Scharfschwerdt, Gerhart von Graevenitz, Michael Beddow, and Monika Schrader have in common the desire to see the Bildungsroman as a highly self-reflective novel, one in which the problem of *Bildung*, of personal growth, is enacted in the narrator's discursive self-understanding rather than in the events which the hero experiences.[4] Schrader, for instance, argues that *Bildung*—the quest for organic growth and personal self-realization—is essentially an epistemological concept and that it finds its exploration within the realm of the specifically narrative (that is, aesthetic) process. For her, the story told is an allegorical field in which the discursively formulated insights can be tried out.

There are many valuable insights to be gained from such an approach. Yet there is also the danger that the Bildungsroman becomes increasingly defined as a discursive essay in the aesthetic mode, whereby the plot, the events chronicled, are relegated to the level of contingent illustrative material. I think that the major Bildungsromane in fact suggest that actual experience is not such a disposable commodity as this. As a result, the Bildungsroman sustains a greater relationship to the traditional *donnée* of the novelist's art than such arguments allow.

[4] Scharfschwerdt, *Thomas Mann und der deutsche Bildungsroman* (Stuttgart, 1967); Graevenitz, *Die Setzung des Subjekts: Untersuchungen zur Romantheorie* (Tübingen, 1973); Beddow, "Thomas Mann's *Felix Krull* and the Traditions of the Picaresque Novel and the Bildungsroman" (Ph.D. diss., Cambridge University, 1975); Schrader, *Mimesis and Poiesis: Poetologische Studien zum Bildungsroman* (Berlin and New York, 1975).

These two conflicting approaches to the Bildungsroman, the "thematic" and the "aesthetic," serve to remind us of an established debate within novel theory: the novel, more than any other literary mode, has been seen as both the vehicle for a massively referential artistic concern, and as a highly structured and *durchkomponiert* aesthetic construct. The novel should, it has been claimed, recreate an existing world, and it should also create its own artistic totality. The debate about the Bildungsroman is, when viewed in this light, part of a longer debate about the novel as such. In more general terms, however, the two schools of Bildungsroman theoreticians can be seen as participants in that literary controversy which is at the forefront of present methodological discussion. I am referring to the battle between Marxists and Structuralists. There is, I think, no need to go into details (or indeed the various subgroups) here. What I have in mind is the conflict between those critics who insist on the referentiality of the work of art and those who insist on its structural integrity—between, at the crudest level of generalization, those for whom the work of art is "about life" and those for whom it is "about itself." I want to suggest in my analysis of the Bildungsroman that, in general terms, the literary work is both referential and self-constituting, that, more specifically, the Bildungsroman is a novel genre which derives its very life from the awareness both of the given experiential framework of practical reality on the one hand and of the creative potential of human imagination and reflectivity on the other. The contemporary methodological debate finds a fascinating thematic correlative in the German Bildungsroman tradition.

One final word about the range of texts treated in this study. I have made a conventional choice in the sense that the six major novels I have selected for detailed analysis would commonly be regarded as the finest

examples of the genre. It should, however, be stressed
that the tradition does not consist only of a few high
points. There are a large number of German novels
which concern themselves with the growth and change
of a young man through adolescence and which take
this period as precisely the one in which decisive intellectual and philosophical issues are embedded in the
psychological process of human self-discovery. Speaking of the growth of intelligence in the adolescent, Roy
Pascal rightly observes: "no novelists have shaped this
process, and the world in which it takes place, so subtly
and tenderly as the Germans."[5] In this context one
thinks of such novels as Karl Philipp Moritz's *Anton
Reiser*, Novalis's *Heinrich von Ofterdingen*, Ludwig
Tieck's *Franz Sternbald's Wanderings*, Jean Paul's *Un-
fledged Years*, Joseph von Eichendorff's *Intimations and the
Present*, Karl Immermann's *The Epigones*, Gustav
Freytag's *Debit and Credit*, Wilhelm Raabe's *The Hunger
Pastor*, Hugo von Hofmannsthal's *Andreas*, Hermann
Hesse's *Demian*, and many others. Such novels constitute the transmission of a particular kind of fictional
concern which is, as it were, the breeding ground for
the high points of the German contribution to the novel
form. What, for me, separates the minor texts from the
major ones is precisely the fact that the great works
meet and explore the thematic possibilities of adolescent
flux and change with a differentiation and generosity
that is lacking in the minor works. Put in more specific
terms, I mean that the great texts sustain the dialectic of
practical social reality on the one hand and the complex
inwardness of the individual on the other, whereas the
minor writers tend (to borrow D. H. Lawrence's term) to
put their thumb in the scales, to load the issue either in
favor of the hero's cherished inwardness or in favor of
the practical accommodation to society. The result is a
number of less than distinguished novels. But on the

[5] Pascal, *The German Novel* (Manchester, 1956), 305.

other hand, the profusion of such novels in Germany maintains the parameters of the novel's concern in such a way that the Bildungsroman is a continuously appropriate generic possibility. Edward McInnes and Hartmut Steinecke have, for example, shown that even in the years 1820-1850, when the pendulum swung toward a concern for the historical and social novel, the Bildungsroman—after the model of Goethe's *Wilhelm Meister*—was never quite dislodged from its prestigious position.[6] Indeed, one has the feeling that the Bildungsroman was a model that could channel the creative efforts of different generations of German writers, of, for example, both Romantics and realists alike. For this reason it is not simply a transient phenomenon on the German literary scene. Rather, the Bildungsroman figures as a vital fictional medium by which the German mind, through all its changing historical contexts, could explore and define itself.

[6] McInnes, "Zwischen *Wilhelm Meister* und *Die Ritter vom Geist*: Zur Auseinandersetzung zwischen Bildungsroman und Sozialroman im 19. Jahrhundert," *DVLG*, 43 (1969), 487ff.; Steinecke, "*Wilhelm Meister* oder *Waverley*? Zur Bedeutung Scotts für das deutsche Romanverständnis der frühen Restaurationszeit," in *Teilnahme und Spiegelung*, ed. B. Allemann (Berlin and New York, 1975), 340ff.

= I =

The Bildungsroman
as a Genre

Any concern with imaginative literature inevitably confronts one with the thorny problem of genre. University
literature departments tend to invoke genre categories
when establishing a syllabus of course offerings, yet
the very currency of genre terms is deceptive, for it
implies—wrongly—that critical consensus has been
achieved on the question of how one should define and
employ the literary genre. In fact, once the genre term is
seen as more than a convenient label, theoretical confusion and uncertainty abound. In one sense, of course,
the argument about the validity of genre concepts is
simply a localized version of the much older philosophical debate about the relationship of the particular
and the general, and for this reason it is hardly surprising that diametrically opposed positions (both nom-
inalist and realist, as it were) continue to be maintained
with equal fervor. Moreover, the debate about literary
genres is compounded by additional complex issues, for
example, those involving the role of individuality in
literary creation, of "genius" versus "tradition,"
thereby further troubling the already muddied waters.

Tzvetan Todorov, in his study of the fantastic, has
raised the important problems with great acuity and cogency. He points out that the concept of genre (or
species) is borrowed from the natural sciences. And he
insists that "there is a qualitative difference as to the
meanings of the term 'genre' or 'specimen,' depending
on whether they are applied to natural beings or to the
works of the mind."[1] "In the former case," he con-

[1] Todorov, *The Fantastic: A Structural Approach to a Literary Genre*
(Cleveland and London, 1973), 5.

tinues, "the appearance of a new example does not necessarily modify the characteristics of the species; consequently, the properties of the new example are for the most part deducible from the pattern of the species. . . . The birth of a new tiger does not modify the species in its definition."[2] But in art, "*every* work modifies the sum of possible works, each new example alters the species."[3] How, then, are we to define the constantly changing artistic species?

Any attempt to analyze the process by which we understand the work of art must, in my view, employ the notion of the hermeneutic circle. This model argues that we understand any new phenomenon by moving in a circle between general and specific. Within any given text, the process of understanding is circular: we can only comprehend the meaning of one line from a poem by assigning it to its context within the overall meaning of the poem. And we can only arrive at that overall meaning by the cumulative understanding of the individual lines. The circular model of the understanding process also informs our relationship to the work in its entirety. When we read a novel, we do so (whether we realize it or not) with certain expectations in mind. These expectations, these predispositions to a certain kind of reading, help to condition, and are in their turn conditioned by, the specific work before us. Hence, our understanding of the individual text is a constant movement between generality and specificity, between notional genre and given work. Moreover, it must be stressed that genre constructs have historical validity: they are not foisted on the works after the event by eagerly taxonomic scholars and readers. Rather, the historical agency of the genre constitutes that "horizon of expectation"[4] with reference to which each individual

---

[2] Ibid., 5-6.
[3] Ibid., 6. See also the discussion of Todorov's theory of genre in *New Literary History*, 8 (1976), 145ff.
[4] H. R. Jauss, *Literaturgeschichte als Provokation* (Frankfurt, 1970), 177.

work is made. This is not, of course, to deny the role of individual creativity. But the specific work activates and energizes those expectations in order to debate with them, to refashion, to challenge, perhaps even to parody them. This is the "newness"—the individuality within the ongoing generality of the literary species—of which Todorov speaks. Indeed, he makes the telling point that only pulp literature fully interlocks with its genre expectation, and that this is the criterion for distinguishing creative from spurious literature: "only 'popular' literature (detective stories, serialized novels, science fiction, etc.) would approach fulfilling the requirements of genre in the sense the word has in natural science: for the notion of genre in that sense would be inapplicable to strictly literary texts."[5]

I want to insist that the notion of generality, of genre, is indispensable to any understanding of literary texts, and that the lifeblood of any genre must be the interrelationship of general expectation and specific praxis, of theoretical corpus and its palpable, individuated (that is, modified) realization in an actual work.[6] It is with this process, as it works in certain German novel fictions from 1767 to 1943, that I shall be concerned in this study.

The theoretical basis of my undertaking can be made clear by contrast with that adopted by Jürgen Jacobs in his study *Wilhelm Meister und seine Brüder: Untersuchungen zum deutschen Bildungsroman*.[7] Jacobs speaks of the Bildungsroman as an "unfulfilled genre."[8] While one knows what Jacobs means—that the Bildungsroman operates with an implied teleology that it only imperfectly fulfills—I believe it is wrong to identify the genre itself with that teleology. In so doing, Jacobs abstracts the notion of genre from its realization in the specific literary work and makes the genre concept

[5] Todorov, *The Fantastic*, 6.
[6] For a more detailed discussion of genre-historicity see my study, *The German Novelle* (Princeton, 1977), 11ff.
[7] (Munich, 1972).   [8] Ibid., 271.

something extraliterary. As Monika Schrader so well puts it: "the praxis of the work of art itself—and not literary theory—must be the starting point and basis for the definition of the literary genre."[9] I want to insist that the genre works *within* individual fictions in that it is a component of the expectation to which the specific novels refer and which they vivify by their creative engagement with it. The degree to which the expectation is or is not fulfilled is not the criterion for participation in the genre construct. As long as the model of the genre is intimated as a sustained and sustaining presence in the work in question, then the genre retains its validity as a structuring principle within the palpable stuff of an individual literary creation. In other words, the notion of a genre must, in my view, operate as a function of the imaginative literature written with reference to that concept; it is not a petrified, extraliterary thing. Even the nonfulfillment of consistently intimated expectation can, paradoxically, represent a validation of the genre by means of its controlled critique. The problematic of the Bildungsroman texts is the *raison d'être* of the genre of which they partake.

The term *Bildungsroman* was first used by Karl Morgenstern in the early 1820s. He defined the genre as follows:

> It will justly bear the name *Bildungsroman* firstly and primarily on account of its thematic material, because it portrays the *Bildung* of the hero in its beginnings and growth to a certain stage of completeness; and also secondly because it is by virtue of this portrayal that it furthers the reader's *Bildung* to a much greater extent than any other kind of novel.[10]

[9] Schrader, *Mimesis und Poiesis* (Berlin and New York, 1975), 3.
[10] Quoted in Lothar Köhn, *Entwicklungs- und Bildungsroman* (Stuttgart, 1969), 5.

This first usage of the term has only recently come to light.[11] In view of the suggestiveness of Morgenstern's comments it is surprising that the term *Bildungsroman* was used only infrequently until the late nineteenth century, when it was, so to speak, put on the map by Dilthey. Since then, the term has enjoyed great currency. This might lead one to conclude that the term—and with it the essential implications of the genre—only acquires resonance *after* the great line of eighteenth- and nineteenth-century Bildungsromane. But I do not believe this is so. The term may not have gained currency until late, but, as I hope to show shortly, many of the implications of the genre are commonplaces within nineteenth-century novel theory in Germany. Morgenstern may have coined the term and summarized some of its possible implications, but the kind of novel he was envisaging had been analyzed before, by the critic Friedrich von Blanckenburg in his *Versuch über den Roman* (*Essay on the Novel*) of 1774. This work of novel theory grew out of Blanckenburg's enthusiasm for a specific work of fiction, Christoph Martin Wieland's *Agathon* (1767), and for the way in which that individual creation is shot through with theoretical implications in that it overtly (and thematically) transforms the traditional novel genre by investing it with a new psychological and intellectual seriousness. The Bildungsroman was born in a remarkable fusion of theory and practice—and with it the German novel came of age. Moreover, as Fritz Martini has shown,[12] Morgenstern's coinage of the term *Bildungsroman* is, like Blanckenburg's treatise, a theoretical response to a particular work of fiction. For Morgenstern, the work which inaugurated the modern novel in all its resonance was Goethe's *Wilhelm Meister's Apprenticeship*.

It is because of this precise historicity of the Bil-

---

[11] See Fritz Martini, "Der Bildungsroman," *DVLG*, 35 (1961), 44ff.
[12] Ibid.

dungsroman genre, expressed in a twofold interlocking of theory and practice, that I intend to use this term, despite the time-lag which afflicts the term itself, in preference to two others with which it has often been felt to be interchangeable: *Erziehungsroman* and *Entwicklungsroman*.[13] I would suggest that the Erziehungsroman is, unlike the Bildungsroman, explicitly (and narrowly) pedagogic in the sense that it is concerned with a certain set of values to be acquired, of lessons to be learned. As I hope to show, the Bildungsroman both in theory and in practice is concerned with a much more diffuse—and therefore more general—process by which the individual grows and evolves. The word *Bildung* implies the generality of a culture, the clustering of values by which a man lives, rather than a specifically *educational* attainment. The term *Entwicklungsroman* is much more general, and it is one which carries less emotive and intellectual ballast than does *Bildungsroman*. I would take the former term to embrace any novel having one central figure whose experiences and whose changing self occupy a role of structural primacy within the fiction. *Entwicklungsroman*, then, is a fairly neutral indicator of a certain kind of fictive organization, whereas *Bildungsroman* is a genre term that has both cultural and philosophical resonance.

I want to argue that the Bildungsroman genre was born in specific historical circumstances, that is, within the *Humanitätsideal* of late eighteenth-century Germany. It is a novel form that is animated by a concern for the whole man unfolding organically in all his complexity and richness. *Bildung* becomes, then, a total growth process, a diffused *Werden*, or becoming, involving something more intangible than the acquirement of a finite number of lessons. Such a concern is the expression of a particular kind of bourgeois humanism, one

[13] On this distinction see François Jost, "La Tradition du Bildungsroman," *Comparative Literature*, 21 (1969), 101ff.

that retains a special (albeit problematic) hold over the German imagination. The centrality of the concept *Bildung*, of the self-realization of the individual in his wholeness, for such figures as Goethe, Schiller, and Wilhelm von Humboldt is well known. The urgency of their concern is a measure of the anguish with which they perceived the growing threat of narrowness and specialization in the society around them. One of the most eloquent statements of that perception comes in a magnificent—and crucial—passage from Schiller's *Letters on the Aesthetic Education of Man*:

> With us, too, the image of the human species is projected in magnified form into separate individuals—but as fragments . . . with the result that in order to get any idea of the totality of human nature one has to go the rounds from individual to individual . . . taking from this one his memory, from that one his tabulating intelligence, from yet another his mechanical skill, and piece them together into a picture of the species. With us it might almost seem as though the various faculties appear as separate in practice as they are distinguished by the psychologist in theory, and we see not merely individuals, but whole classes of men, developing but one of their potentialities, while of the rest, as in stunted plants, only vestigial traces remain. . . . Enjoyment has become divorced from labour, the means from the end, the effort from the reward. Everlastingly chained to a single little fragment of the whole, man himself develops into nothing but a fragment. . . . Thus little by little the concrete life of the individual is destroyed in order that the abstract idea of the whole may drag out its sorry existence.[14]

[14] Schiller, *On the Aesthetic Education of Man: In a Series of Letters*, ed. and trans. E. M. Wilkinson and L. A. Willoughby (Oxford, 1967), 33ff. For a discussion of the classical theory of *Bildung* see: E. L. Stahl, *Die*

Such concerns were not confined to the great artists. One must also stress that many of the implications of the Bildungsroman have their roots not simply in specifically cultural concerns of the last decades of the eighteenth century, but also in a much broader complex of intellectual currents. Dilthey, in his essay *The Eighteenth Century and the Historical World*, stressed the importance of historicism for the eighteenth century. On one level, this historicism is the espousal of a universal principle in that it upholds a powerful teleological force as the motive power of universal history; on another level (with, say, Herder), it involves a recognition of the specificity of historical change, a realization that the growth and evolution of man are interlocked with quite particular social and geographical circumstances. These two strands within historicism are, Dilthey argued, a potent legacy to the nineteenth century. They also, as we shall see, find their way into the Bildungsroman. Indeed, for much nineteenth-century German thinking, history is the vital domain in which idea and empirical reality, spirit and the contingencies of given social context, interact. The tensions in German historiography from Dilthey onward have been well documented by Carlo Antoni in his important study, *From History to Sociology*.[15] The conflict between the principles of materialistic relativism and of metaphysical self-realization, between, to shift the concepts but not the ground of the debate, *Naturwissenschaften* (natural sciences) and *Geisteswissenschaften* (sciences of the mind, that is, the humanities), is a vital issue in the intellectual life of nineteenth-century Germany, and it is one whose roots extend back to the age in which the Bildungsroman was

---

religiöse und die humanitätsphilosophische Bildungsidee und die Entstehung des Bildungsromans im 18. Jahrhundert (Bern, 1934); W. H. Bruford, *The German Tradition of Self-Cultivation* (Cambridge, 1975); and Wilkinson and Willoughby's superb introduction to Schiller's *Aesthetic Education of Man*.
[15] (London, 1962).

born.[16] The Bildungsroman, like any novel, is concerned with the *history* of its hero. This history is enacted within the finite realm of social practicality, and it also partakes of the infinite realm of his inwardness, of his human potentiality. Immanuel Kant, in his *Ideas for General History in a Cosmopolitan Sense* (1784), sketched for his readers the general process by which man, in fulfilling his nature, obeys that teleology which is embedded in the species to which he belongs. Kant insisted that the species eventually "works its way up to the condition in which all seeds which nature has planted can be fully developed, and the human species can fulfill its destiny on earth."[17] Here one senses a general, programmatic statement of that *Bildung* whose operation in the life of one individual the Bildungsroman seeks to document. In a fascinating aside Kant at one point asks whether he is truly offering history, given that he is, by definition, talking of that which has not yet been realized: "It is admittedly a surprising, and to all appearances wayward, undertaking to attempt the composition of a *history* according to some idea of how the world ought to evolve if it is to be in accord with certain rational goals. It would seem that such an intention could only produce a novel."[18] It is indeed at the intersection of story (history) and mind (idea) that the Bildungsroman will generate its characteristic import, one which evolves out of an artistically controlled, and frequently unresolved, tension.

The finest discussion of these issues in terms specific to novel fiction is to be found in Blanckenburg's *Essay on*

---

[16] For an admirable discussion of these issues see Peter Hans Reill, *The German Enlightenment and the Rise of Historicism* (Berkeley and London, 1975).

[17] Kant, *Was ist Aufklärung? Aufsätze zur Geschichte und Philosophie*, ed. J. Zehbe (Göttingen, 1967), 53.

[18] Ibid., 52. On the hermeneutics of the novel's relationship to history see H. V. Geppert, *Der "andere" historische Roman* (Tübingen, 1976).

the Novel.[19] His theory emerges as the recognition of a
specific literary achievement, the first edition of Wieland's *Agathon*. Blanckenburg's criticism derives its cogency from the fact that Wieland's fiction is overtly *also* a
work of novel theory.[20] *Agathon* engages the reader
again and again in a debate about the nature of novel
fictions—and about their applicability to the case which
this novel puts before us. Indeed, it is because *Agathon*
is a novel which takes issue with conventional norms of
novel writing that it is for Blanckenburg a serious artistic
achievement. What Wieland repudiates by implication
is the romance which so long-windedly fuses love story
and adventure novel: a pair of constant lovers is separated at the beginning of the novel, then go through all
manner of episodic adventures, only to be reunited at
the end. For Blanckenburg, Wieland's signal achievement resides in his ability to get inside a character, to
portray the complex stuff of human potential which, in
interaction with the outside world, yields the palpable
process of living and changing. Because Wieland's

[19] Blanckenburg's theory was not, of course, the only significant
eighteenth-century perception of the potential resonance of the novel
form. But where previous novel theoreticians were groping with the
fluidity and pluralism of the genre, Blanckenburg was, I think, the
first to grasp the overall significance and range of its aesthetic possibilities. See for example the valuable compilation, *Theorie und Technik
des Romans im 17. und 18. Jahrhundert*, ed. D. Kimpel and C.
Wiedemann, I (Tübingen, 1970).

[20] In one sense, as Ernst Weber has so cogently shown in *Die
poetologische Selbstreflexion im deutschen Roman des 18. Jahrhunderts*
(Stuttgart, 1974), Wieland's achievement in writing an overtly self-
reflective novel is indebted to many previous novel fictions in Germany. Wieland was not, as it were, the creator *ex nihilo* of the modern
novel. But he was surely (as was Blanckenburg in theoretical terms)
the first to perceive the full resonance of the various devices of narrative self-commentary which he inherited. See also Gotthold Ephraim
Lessing's enthusiastic review of *Agathon* in the *Hamburgische
Dramaturgie*, December 29, 1767. On the specifically aesthetic implications of Wieland's novel see Schrader, *Mimesis und Poiesis*, 133ff. For a
discussion of Wieland's linguistic achievement see Eric A. Blackall,
The Emergence of German as a Literary Language (Cambridge, 1959), 410ff.

novel shows this process, this *Werden*, it confers artistic—and human—dignity and cohesion on that sequence of adventures through which the hero passes. Moreover, it is this process in all its complexity that matters, on which narrative time, energy, and interest is expended, and not the celebration of any goal which can thereby be attained. Blanckenburg senses the profound resonance of *Agathon*, a resonance which one can gauge from the following entry in Johann Georg Sulzer's *General Theory of the Fine Arts* (Leipzig, 1773-1775). There is, significantly, no entry under *novel*, only the following gloss on the adjective *novelistic*: "Thus one describes whatever in content, tone, or expression bears the characteristics which prevailed in earlier novels—such as fondness for adventures, stiltedness in actions, events, feelings. The natural is more or less the exact opposite of the novelistic."[21] If, then, the German novel comes of age with *Agathon*, it does so by breaking with, or, more accurately, by reshaping and deepening, past norms and by demonstrating an intense and sustained concern for the growth of an individual in all his experiential complexity and potentiality. It would seem, then, that it is precisely this interest in the inner life and processes of the individual which confers poetic seriousness on what was hitherto an improbable narrative of colorful episodic events.

The modern German novel was born—but not without, as it were, a "bad conscience."[22] The novel, it seems, retains that questionable legacy of being largely events, adventures, episodes, and little (or no) human and poetic substance. Looking at subsequent theories of the novel in Germany, one has the impression that the

[21] Quoted in *Theorie und Technik*, ed. Kimpel and Wiedemann, I, 144.

[22] For an admirable historical documentation of that "bad conscience" and of inwardness as the redemption of novel fiction see Albert Ward, *Book Production, Fiction, and the German Reading Public 1740-1800* (Oxford, 1974), esp. 11ff.

novel, as a genre, stands in constant need of rehabilitation. That rehabilitation and what it entails was expressed with almost monotonous intensity in German novel theory throughout the nineteenth century, and it was nearly always formulated as a concern for the achievement of *poetry* within the novel: the danger with the novel is that it so easily backslides into the condition of *prose*. The paradigmatic statement is to be found in Georg Wilhelm Friedrich Hegel's comments on the novel in his *Aesthetics*:

> This novelistic quality is born when the knightly existence is again taken seriously, is filled out with real substance. The contingency of outward, actual existence has been transformed into the firm, secure order of bourgeois society and the state, so that now the police, the law courts, the army occupy the position of those chimerical goals which the knight used to set himself. Thereby the knightly character of those heroes whose deeds fill recent novels is transformed. They stand as individuals with their subjective goals of love, honor, ambition or with their ideals of improving the world, over against the existing order and prose of reality which from all sides places obstacles in their path. . . . Especially young men are these new knights who have to make their way, and who regard it as a misfortune that there are in any shape or form such things as family, bourgeois society. . . . It is their aim to punch a hole in this order of things, to change the world. . . . These struggles are, however, in the modern world nothing but the apprenticeship, the education of the individual at the hands of the given reality. . . . For the conclusion of such an apprenticeship usually amounts to the hero getting the corners knocked off him. . . . In the last analysis he usually gets his girl and some kind of

job, marries and becomes a philistine just like the others.[23]

This is, it seems to me, a crucial passage, not just for the perceptions it offers of the nature of the novel genre, but also for its essential ambivalence. On the one hand, Hegel affirms the seriousness of this kind of novel fiction, a seriousness which derives from its ability to anchor the time-honored epic pattern in modern bourgeois reality. In this sense, Hegel seems to offer approval of that process by which the world prevails over the hero's dreams, desires, and fantasies to the point where the somewhat fastidious, idealistic young man is licked into shape and taught to affirm society and all it stands for. Yet on the other hand, Hegel also suggests that there is something debased, and debasing, about this process. That the highest wisdom of the novel—and of its latter-day knightly adventurer—should reside in the acquirement of wife, family, and job security seems a sorry reduction of the grand model. The ambivalence is, of course, characteristic of much of Hegel's thinking: on the one hand, contemporary reality is apostrophized as the finest, most rational self-realization of the world spirit in its historical workings; on the other hand, that given reality is but a phase with a built-in impetus toward self-transcendence. The hedging of bets in regard to prosaic bourgeois reality is characteristic not only of Hegel himself, but also, as we shall see, of the Bildungsroman genre. And the uncertainty becomes nowhere more apparent, as Hegel perceived, than in the vexed problem of the novel's ending.

In another passage from the *Aesthetics* Hegel makes clear that the original impetus to epic writing was a

---

[23] Hegel, *Vorlesungen über die Ästhetik*, ed. F. Bassenge (Berlin, 1955), 557-58. Hegel's ambivalence is discussed in Hans Hiebel, *Individualität und Totalität: Zur Geschichte des bürgerlichen Poesiebegriffs* (Bonn, 1974), 284ff.

sense of the magic and poetry of the world. Yet modern society presupposes "a reality already ordered into *prose*, on the basis of which it [the novel] reattains for poetry its lost rights."[24] Hence, Hegel continues, the central conflict in the modern novel is that "between the poetry of the heart and the resisting prose of circumstances."[25] Some kind of reconciliation can, apparently, be effected: the world of prose can be made to lose some of its hard edges and to allow for a validation of the poetry of the heart. And Hegel insists that this area of validation, this room for aesthetic maneuver, must be granted particularly to that artist who is committed to rendering the prose of real life "without himself remaining enmeshed in the realm of the prosaic and the everyday."[26]

The issues Hegel raised, which can be summarized under the heading of "poetic" versus "prosaic" modes of being and of artistic creation, can be traced through the theoretical remarks on the novel made by Friedrich Schleiermacher (1819-1832), Karl Immermann (1826), Arthur Schopenhauer (1851), Karl Gutzkow (1855), Friedrich Theodor Vischer (1857), Otto Ludwig (1860), Friedrich Spielhagen (1874), and Gustav Freytag (1886). They are commonplaces within nineteenth-century novel theory in Germany, and they reflect that unease about the novel genre that informs Wieland's *Agathon* and Blanckenburg's *Essay on the Novel*. This ongoing bad conscience accounts, in my view, for the fact that one specific version of the novel, the Bildungsroman, became the dominant mode for the major narrative talents of German literature. I have no wish to claim that Germans are congenitally incapable of writing novels other than Bildungsromane. On the other hand, the fact remains that most German novel writing of distinction

[24] Hegel, *Vorlesungen über die Ästhetik*, 983.
[25] Ibid.   [26] Ibid.

partakes of this genre construct and that the distinction derives from the artistic resonance with which dominant social, intellectual, psychological, and cultural concerns are taken up and explored. It is part of the historicity of the genre that on its first emergence it was hailed as giving respectability to a debased literary mode, as legitimating and redeeming the popular form by marrying the traditional episodic and providential plot with a thoroughgoing concern for the experiential potentiality of the central character. Thomas Mann suggested as much when he wrote that the Bildungsroman is the "sublimation and rendering inward of the novel of adventures."[27]

What precisely is meant here? At the simplest level, one should note that the Bildungsroman is a novel which gives dignity to the creaky mechanics of a providential plot by suggesting that the adventures that befall the hero and the people he meets are significant insofar as they strike an answering chord in him, as they are part of his potentiality. If this is the case, it follows that the characters and experiences are allowed to recur because they are abidingly present in the selfhood of the hero. The Bildungsroman, with its concern for the *Werden* of an individual, is able—in Hegel's and so many theoreticians' terms—to redeem the prosaic facticity of the given social world by relating it to the inner potentialities of the hero. It is a novel form which esteems possibilities as much as actualities; indeed, at times it runs the risk of esteeming actualities only insofar as they are validated and underwritten by the hero's inwardness. It is surely for this reason, for the mediation between "poetic" and "prosaic," that the Bildungsroman became such a central model for novel writing in

[27] Mann, "Die Kunst des Romans," in *Schriften und Reden zur Literatur, Kunst, und Philosophie*, ed. H. Bürgin, II (Frankfurt, 1968), 357.

Germany in the late eighteenth and the nineteenth centuries, and indeed, even into the twentieth. [28] It is worth noting here that one novel, above all others, was the object of immediate and thoroughgoing critical debate, a debate which marked out the vital issues in such a way as to make that text and its reception almost a paradigm for all that followed. I am thinking, of course, of Goethe's *Wilhelm Meister's Apprenticeship*. I will consider the text itself in a later chapter. But the reception and discussion to which it gave rise must be documented in any discussion of German novel theory. Two phases of the reception of *Wilhelm Meister* are particularly important: first, the interchange of letters involving Goethe, Schiller, Humboldt, and Christian Gottfried Körner; and second, the Romantic reaction, as exemplified by Friedrich Schlegel and Novalis. It is noteworthy that Goethe himself expressed considerable uncertainty about his own novel. To Johann Peter Eckermann he commented: "People look for a center, and that is hard—and not even good."[29] But at times he was prepared to formulate some kind of overall idea, "that man in spite of all his stupidity and confusions does, guided by some higher hand, yet attain a happy goal."[30]

This unease about the central idea of the novel is the mainspring of the exchange of letters between Goethe and Schiller. Schiller, as Klaus Gille points out in his indispensable book,[31] consistently suggested that *Wilhelm Meister* is too tentative in its handling of the underlying

[28] Ralph Freedman, in his admirable study *The Lyrical Novel* (Princeton, 1963), sees the genre with which he is concerned as one heavily embedded in the German novel tradition. For a discussion of the unease in German novel theory, but within a different conceptual framework, see Beatrice Wehrli, *Imitatio und Mimesis in der Geschichte der deutschen Erzähltheorie* (Göttingen, 1974).

[29] *Goethes Werke*, ed. Erich Trunz et al. (Hamburg, 1948-1960), VIII, 520 (hereafter cited as *Hamburger Ausgabe*).

[30] Ibid.

[31] Gille, *Wilhelm Meister im Urteil der Zeitgenossen* (Assen, 1971), 17ff.

idea, an idea which for Schiller was the development
(*Bildung*) of the hero toward some state of (aesthetic)
wholeness. The correspondence revolves around the
tension between what Schiller called his "whim concerning the clearer enunciation of the principal idea,"[32]
and Goethe's obliqueness in the novel. As Goethe himself admitted to Schiller: "the flaw which you quite
rightly notice comes from my innermost nature—from a
certain realistic tic."[33] One notes the tact and good
humor with which the disagreement was aired. The
conciliatory tone derives, I think, not simply from the
formal yet cordial relations that prevailed between the
two men, but also from the specific object under discussion. Schiller called his concern for a clearer idea a
Grille, a whim, and Goethe acknowledged the lack of
clear-cut idea to be a "flaw" and attributed it to his
"realistic tic." Each man, by implication, recognized the
other's position as a valid counterweight to his own
idiosyncratic preferences ("whim," "tic"). Each response emerges in the debate as but one pole within the
necessary interpretative dialectic generated by this, in
Goethe's term,[34] "incalculable" novel.

One notes how wonderfully perceptive are Schiller's
comments on *Wilhelm Meister*. He was able to be
genuinely appreciative of precisely those qualities in the
novel which would seem to be the source of his reservations. He observed that Wilhelm "achieves definiteness,
without losing his lovely openness to redefinition,"[35]
and that the "idea of mastery cannot and may not stand
as his purpose and goal *before* him [Wilhelm] . . . rather
it must stand as leader *behind* him."[36] What Schiller acknowledged in such remarks is the tentativeness of
Goethe's novel, a tentativeness born of that "realistic
tic" which prevents the novel from becoming the

---

[32] *Hamburger Ausgabe*, viii, 549.   [33] Ibid., 542-43.
[34] Ibid., 520.   [35] Ibid., 542.
[36] Ibid., 540.

overtly allegorical embodiment of certain "ideal" energies. We are, in other words, concerned with a tentative process, one in which (to use the terms implicit in Kant's *Ideas for General History in a Cosmopolitan Sense*) there is a tension between history and teleology, between actuality and notionality, between pattern constructed after the event and shaping purpose known in advance of its self-realization. The openness, the obliqueness of Goethe's novel is, as I hope to show in my detailed analysis, the deepest source of the book's meaning. Its resonant oscillation between idea and reality is enacted in the Goethe-Schiller correspondence, and this gives meaning to Goethe's remark of 1815 about that correspondence, referring to it as "the great achievement which Schiller and I managed: to continue uninterruptedly a common *Bildung* despite our totally divergent directions."[37] Thus the process explored in the novel was apparently continued in the exchange of letters: the divergent directions were the necessary response to the informing dialectic of the novel and to the issues it raised.

One further insight emerges from this correspondence. In November 1796 Schiller wrote to Goethe commenting on the nature of the main character and of his function within the fiction as a whole. In so doing he took up observations made by both Körner and Humboldt. Körner had insisted (and Gille suggests that he was arguing under the impact of Blanckenburg's novel theory)[38] on the primacy of Wilhelm as the harmoniously developing, individual hero, whereas Humboldt had suggested that the novel functioned "completely independently of any particular individuality."[39] Once again, two differing positions adopted vis-à-vis the novel text precisely uncover a significant dialectic. Schiller took up the differing viewpoints and suggested the

[37] Ibid., III, 305. [38] Gille, *Wilhelm Meister*, 38-39.
[39] *Hamburger Ausgabe*, VIII, 553.

interlocking of both perceptions within the characterization of Wilhelm. Wilhelm is, in other words, both an individual character with a specific life-history and also a reservoir of human potentiality: "It is, of course, a delicate and awkward aspect of this novel, that, in the figure of Meister, it closes neither with a consistent individuality nor with a consistent ideality, but with a mixture of the two."[40] I shall have occasion to refer at greater length to this problem of character in the Bildungsroman. Suffice it to say at this stage that, as far as I am aware, the insights contributed by Schiller, Körner, and Humboldt have not been surpassed (indeed, they have seldom been equaled) by modern criticism of the Bildungsroman.

The Romantic reaction to *Wilhelm Meister* is significant in that it involves a restatement and deepening of many of the issues raised by the Goethe-Schiller correspondence. Friedrich Schlegel perceived the great historical significance of the novel, seeing it as one of the "tendencies" (albeit imperfectly fulfilled)[41] of the age. In his *Athenäum* review (1798) he praised the irony of the novel, the way in which Goethe's narrative skill dissolves the weight and seriousness of prosaic facticity through a perspective of ironic detachment. He saw the novel as self-reflective, integrating discursive elements into its narrative flow: the novel is, then, "pure, high poetry" in that it is witty, alert, and agile, a kind of essayism of the spirit.[42] In his later (1808) review of *Wilhelm Meister*, Schlegel repeated his vindication of the novel's poetic essence, but added an acknowledgment of its didactic aim, which derives from the concept of *Bildung* as "a mediator between emotion and reason, . . . which encompasses both."[43] Schlegel, then, could cherish the novel for its obliqueness *and* its didacticism, for its irony *and* its high cultural and moral concern. At

---

[40] Ibid., 551.
[41] See Gille, *Wilhelm Meister*, 101.
[42] *Hamburger Ausgabe*, VIII, 559.
[43] Ibid., 569.

one level, of course, one can see the change in emphasis
as a function of Schlegel's own personal and intellectual
development between 1798 and 1808. But at another
level, we must recognize that both positions are appropriate to *Wilhelm Meister* and to its responsiveness to different readings.

An oscillation between two responses also characterizes Novalis's comments on *Wilhelm Meister*. Up to
about 1800 Novalis's assessment is positive in that he
praised the irony, the sheer poetry with which Goethe
handled banal and everyday material. But then he
changed his evaluation drastically: in a bitter outburst
he denounced the novel as "a *Candide* aimed at poetry,"
as "utterly prosaic and modern."[44] Once again, it must
be stressed that Novalis's change of heart was not mere
inconsistency on his part. The very terms of his argument make his voice one among many within nineteenth-century novel theory in Germany. And perhaps
Wilhelm Meister is the archetypal Bildungsroman in the
sense that it focuses with paradigmatic energy on a
whole number of issues concerning plot, individual development, and the selfhood of the hero, concerning
above all else the poetry of the heart (inwardness and
potentiality) vis-à-vis the unyielding, prosaic temporality of practical social existence. It is no accident that
most nineteenth-century novel theory in Germany
seems to be a running commentary on the Bildungsroman and, more specifically, on Goethe's *Wilhelm
Meister*.

It has been stressed over and over again that the Bildungsroman is a novel form that is unremittingly concerned with the *Werden* of an individual hero. One
needs to ask how this process is intimated narratively
and how it embodies the dialectic of "poetry" and
"prose." The passage already quoted from Hegel is particularly suggestive here. In terms of its portrayal of the

[44] Ibid., 571.

hero, the Bildungsroman operates with a tension between a concern for the sheer complexity of individual potentiality on the one hand and a recognition on the other that practical reality—marriage, family, career—is a necessary dimension of the hero's self-realization, albeit one that by definition implies a delimitation, indeed, a constriction, of the self. The tension is that between the *Nebeneinander* (the "one-alongside-another") of possible selves within the hero and the *Nacheinander* (the "one-after-another") of linear time and practical activity, that is, between potentiality and actuality. This tension is, it seems to me, central to the process of thematic argument of the Bildungsroman. Michael Beddow, in his perceptive study of the Bildungsroman, argues that the genre is essentially an epic of inwardness, one that celebrates the imagination of the hero as the faculty which allows him to transcend the limitations of everyday practicality.[45] In this sense, Beddow argues, the Bildungsroman stresses its own fictionality, stresses that it is a product of the human imagination, and thereby establishes an alternative model to the prevailing social reality. There is, I think, great cogency to Beddow's contention, but I feel that he makes the genre too unproblematic in that he stresses one side of the dialectic I have described, to the obliteration of its other pole. The major novels of the tradition are, it seems to me, not simply allegories of the inner life. Practical reality continues to impinge on the cherished inwardness of the hero, and precisely this process is the source of the irony, the obliqueness, the uncertainty which so many commentators have noticed. It is, moreover, the same

[45] Beddow, "Thomas Mann's *Felix Krull* and the Traditions of the Picaresque Novel and the Bildungsroman" (Ph.D. diss., Cambridge University, 1975). Beddow's definition of the Bildungsroman (pp. 11ff.) would overlap with Freedman's notion of the lyrical novel (*Lyrical Novel*, 28). Freedman acknowledges the significance of the Bildungsroman tradition for the lyrical novel, but stresses that the Bildungsroman involves a greater admixture of the traditional realistic novel epistemology than is to be found in the lyrical novel.

process that makes the "learning from life" which the hero undergoes such a tentative progression. Over and over again, the novels themselves pose the question of whether the hero has achieved any kind of worthwhile goal or insight. The notion of organic growth, of a maturing process that somehow eludes even conceptual terms, is a difficult one to pinpoint in terms of un-equivocal narrative realization. Perhaps we are essen-tially concerned with an article of faith that seeks to as-sert the reconcilability of human wholeness on the one hand and the facts of limited and limiting social experi-ence on the other. This would be characteristic of the late eighteenth century when the genre emerged; but it should not mislead us into seeing comfortable solutions where the novel itself can only offer directions, implica-tions, and intimations of the possible.

Reading the major novels of the tradition (even its eighteenth-century exemplars), one is persistently struck by the pervasive tentativeness of the narrative undertaking. This precariousness, this hedging of bets, issues in an uncertain relationship to lived experience, whereby the linearity of plot on occasion gives way to symbolically patterned recurrence. Many critics have noted the lack of edge, of once-and-for-all finality in the treatment of human action and interaction in the Bil-dungsroman. Secondary characters are allowed to dis-appear and reappear in a remarkably providential way; they are rarely "lost" because they are relatable to the hero's potentiality. Hence, they are frequently waiting in the wings, available when the hero needs them. Ul-timately, many of them may prove to be related to him or to each other. It is, then, characteristic of the Bil-dungsroman genre that it embodies a skepticism about the law of linear experience. And thereby it tends, in part a least, to call into question that dimension of human self-realization that is activity and actuality, a dimension that is embodied by plot in realistic novel fic-

tions. This *Nacheinander* of linear experience is acknowledged in the Bildungsroman, but with considerable,
often discursively formulated, reservations. The
Nacheinander often emerges, in Robert Musil's phrase, as
the "law of life which, overburdened and dreaming of
simplicity, one longs for."[46] That law, like its aesthetic
correlative, plot, may be an escapist fiction, a cosy dissolving of human complexity into interpretatively unproblematic causality. Musil is, of course, particularly
radical in his argumentation. One remembers the famous reflections on character in *The Man Without Qualities*, where it is suggested that character is most truly a
reservoir of unrealized potentiality rather than a finite
sum of knowable actualities. The inhabitant of a country, we are told, has at least nine characters, dependent
upon his profession, nationality, class, sex, and so on.
But he also has a tenth character: "and this is nothing
but the passive fantasy of unfilled spaces: it allows the
man everything—but with one exception. He cannot
take seriously what his at least nine other characters do
and what happens to them."[47] Thus the essential character of the man would be the inward, unrealized self,
the "player of roles which belong to him as little as do
the laws of the country in which he lives."[48] In many
ways, Musil's conclusions go far beyond those of the
major Bildungsroman novelists in that he withdraws,
both in philosophical and aesthetic terms, any allegiance to plot, to those specifics through which the
self realizes itself in activity.[49] Nonetheless, the questions raised by his novel are also urgent intimations
from the Bildungsroman tradition.

[46] Musil, *Der Mann ohne Eigenschaften* (Reinbek bei Hamburg, 1952),
665.

[47] Ibid., 35.

[48] Ralf Dahrendorf, *Pfade aus Utopia* (Munich, 1967), 182.

[49] Monika Schrader has accorded a central place to Musil within the
Bildungsroman tradition, leading her, in my view, to make the genre
more discursive and allegorical than it is (*Mimesis und Poiesis*, 180ff.).

It is important to stress, however, that unlike *The Man Without Qualities*, the Bildungsroman texts with which I shall here be concerned work with a relationship to plot, to story, which, for all its tentativeness, is retained intact. In one sense, of course, the relatability of the world of external action to the growth and unfolding of the hero's selfhood can imply an insufficient recognition of the chain of cause and effect within practical affairs. That is to say, the Bildungsroman too rarely operates with a precise sense of the moral integrity and otherness of the people with whom the protagonist comes into contact. There can be something rarefied about the Bildungsroman, a sense that the community with which the hero is to be reconciled is not rendered mimetically; rather, it is intimated through the conceptual cohesion of the novelist's fiction, through the writer's collusion with *his* artistic community of notional readers. In other words, it is the *reader* who is initiated into the wholeness and complexity of *Bildung*; the hero and the world through which he moves are only redeemable through the symbolic transformations made possible by an artistic labor of love.

But this is only part of the import generated by the major Bildungsromane which I shall examine. Indeed, these works are remarkable because they do not reach the point of dissolving all relationship to plot, to the *Nacheinander* that is the story. In one sense, they seem to promise just such an obliteration of the flow of resistantly linear experience. Yet, in another sense, they seem unable to break faith with the novel form and to offer an epistemological or aesthetic treatise. The novels themselves remind us that however much the protagonist craves to know only a beneficent reality that will not resist the "poetry" of his selfhood, reality, the law of linearity, will not be gainsaid. Indeed, the Bildungsromane suggest that there is an inalienable need in man to have a story, to know himself as part of that linear flow of experience which cannot be halted at will. For it is the story which binds together contingencies into the weighty sequence of a human destiny. As Barbara Hardy has so well put it, the narrative storyline is not just "an aesthetic invention used by artists to control, manipulate, and order experience, but it is a primary act of mind transferred from life itself. . . . In order really to live, we make up stories about ourselves and others."[50] The story, then, becomes the guarantor that one is living. Obliteration of the story may seem to promise the realization of human wholeness, but ultimately it is a wholeness bought at the unacceptable price of stasis, bloodlessness, death. Moreover, as W. B. Gallie reminds us, the story, like human history, is founded in the attempt to deal with contingencies "by rendering these contingencies acceptable."[51] All of this, Gallie reflects, may not be philosophically respectable. But then the novel, like history, is not a philosophical tract.

Compared with the major exemplars of realistic fiction, the plot of the Bildungsroman, of course, always tends to feel somewhat feeble and half-hearted. But in the context of its own narrative implication, the allegiance to story in the Bildungsroman, however tentative, is quite remarkable. And the tentativeness is offset by a gain: the Bildungsroman is able to offer a critique of those cherished human presuppositions explored by Frank Kermode in his study, *The Sense of an Ending*.[52] It allows the novel to concern itself with a definition of experience which precludes any simple sense of finality, of "over and done with." Of course, the notion of a goal still has a place within human affairs. Yet, ultimately,

[50] Hardy, "Towards a Poetics of Fiction: An Approach through Narrative," *Novel*, 2 (1968), 5.

[51] Gallie, *Philosophy and the Historical Understanding* (London, 1964), 29.

[52] (New York, 1968).

the meaning of the growth process, of the *Werden*, is to be found in the process itself, not in any goal whose attainment it may make possible. The grasping for clarity and losing it, the alternation of certainty of purpose with a sense of the overriding randomness of living, these are seen to be the very stuff of human experience and such meaning and distinction as men are able to attain. The Bildungsroman, then, is written for the sake of the journey, and not for the sake of the happy ending toward which that journey points.[53]

This obliqueness of the German Bildungsroman (a quality Schiller discerned in Goethe's *Wilhelm Meister*) separates the genre from other comparable novel fictions. In his study of the English novel from Dickens to Golding, Jerome H. Buckley persuasively uses the model of the Bildungsroman as his organizing framework.[54] What emerges from his study, however, is that the English novel of adolescence is essentially concerned to find a certain practical accommodation between the hero and the social world around him. Buckley's sketch of the genre could apply to the major German exemplars, except that it fails to allow for the problematic elusiveness of so many of the texts I have chosen for study here. This is not, of course, to raise objections to Buckley's study, which is concerned with another and very different novel tradition. But it is worth noting that the English fiction he examines offers a far greater allegiance to plot, to actuality, to the linear growth of the hero to some kind of adult clarity, than does the German Bildungsroman. Moreover, the English novel of adolescence (*Great Expectations, The Way of*

[53] For a discussion of the problematic ending see Gerda Röder, *Glück und glückliches Ende im deutschen Bildungsroman* (Munich, 1968), and E. Lämmert, "Zum Wandel der Geschichtserfahrung im Reflex der Romantheorie," in *Geschichte: Ereignis und Erzählung*, ed. R. Koselleck and W. Stempel (Munich, 1973).

[54] Buckley, *Season of Youth: The Bildungsroman from Dickens to Golding* (Cambridge, Mass., 1974).

All Flesh, Jude the Obscure, Clayhanger, Portrait of the Artist as a Young Man) operates with a precisely articulated and documented sense of the specific pressures—societal, institutional, psychological—which militate against the hero's quest for self-fulfillment. Such kinds of resistance are rarely portrayed in the German Bildungsroman with any bite or urgency. The forces which oppose its hero are less susceptible of realistic portrayal for the reason that they tend to be ontologically, rather than socially, based. The resistance ranged against the Bildungsroman hero is not a tyrannical parent, not social or economic sanctions; rather, it is the limitations set to any and every existence within the sphere of outward, practical being (however beneficently organized that sphere may be). At several points in his study of the English Bildungsroman Buckley outlines the relationship of English writers to Goethe's *Wilhelm Meister*. Once again, Goethe's novel provokes a highly revealing critical disagreement. It is praised for its openness, its questioning—and is also condemned for its vagueness and bloodlessness. These are hardly original responses. Once again they allow one to conclude that the lifeblood of *Wilhelm Meister*, and of the genre which it so persuasively embodies, is consistently sustained irresolution.

One final thematic concern of the Bildungsroman should be mentioned here, the nature and the limitations of human consciousness. It is tempting in view of the implied but so rarely realized teleology of so much Bildungsroman narration to define the goal pursued by the hero as that of greater, or more perfect, consciousness. Frequently, however, we find that the novels themselves are much more subtle, even evasive, than this. Often we are shown that consciousness is a function of being and that being (specific existence) is in its turn a function of the characters' embeddedness in a given psychological or social context. It follows, then, that neither "consciousness" nor "activity" are separate realms which man can choose to enter or leave. Rather, he inhabits both in their interdependence. The major novels within the Bildungsroman tradition recognize this. Where such is not the case, where novels operate with the simple model of an intact, private self that may choose to enter experience or not, then they succumb to what J. P. Stern has criticized as "the taint of a chimerical freedom—as though somehow it were possible *not* to enter the river of experience that flows all one way."[55] But the major achievements of the tradition do, in my view, suggest that the protagonist's capacity for reflection is part of the whole living process in which he is embedded: it neither antedates nor postdates his actual experiences, but is of a piece with them. Hence, intellectual learning never abidingly transcends the limitations of the hero's life and selfhood. To take two obvious examples, it seems to me essential to recognize that in both Goethe's *Wilhelm Meister* and Thomas Mann's *The Magic Mountain* the seeming goal or "Grail" of both novels—the admission to the Society of the Tower in one, the snow vision in the other—is, as it were, taken back by the ongoing movement of the plot. In both cases we are concerned with a kind of privileged moment, where the possibility of human wholeness is glimpsed, is even discursively formulated. Yet this wholeness is not simply a set of wise sayings which, once learned, guarantee the inalienable possession of that wholeness they intimate. Rather, that wholeness, if it exists anywhere, informs the very flux of a character's life and experience. Wilhelm Meister finds himself clutching a set of maxims but feeling no wiser than before; Hans Castorp totters back to the sanatorium where he forgets those lessons he has affirmed with such conviction.

The Bildungsroman, both in theory and in practice, is little known outside Germany. This is unfortunate,

[55] Stern, *Idylls and Realities* (London, 1971), 132.

specifically because many developments within the twentieth-century novel help us to see the Bildungsroman for the unique and challenging fictional mode that it is. In 1950 Nathalie Sarraute commented on the response of the modern reader to traditional novel fictions: "Quant au caractère il [the reader] sait bien qu'il n'est pas autre chose que l'étiquette grossière dont lui-même se sert, sans trop y croire, pour la commodité pratique, pour régler, en três gros, ses conduites . . . les personnages, tels que les concevait le vieux roman . . . ne parviennent plus à contenir la réalité psychologique actuelle."[56] I wonder whether the "vieux roman" here could possibly include the Bildungsroman from *Agathon* onward. I would beg leave to doubt it. I might add that Sarraute's remark was quoted in a paper on André Gide's novel *Les Faux-Monnayeurs* in which the writer referred to "the twentieth-century devaluation of character" in the novel,[57] and summarized Gide's position by arguing that for Gide, character as traditionally defined is constriction, "is in opposition to something else in human beings which we might call possibility: when a role becomes a man's reality, this possibility or *disponibilité* is destroyed."[58] For readers of the German Bildungsroman these are, I would suggest, familiar considerations.

[56] Sarraute, *L'Ere du Soupçon*, quoted in Catherine Savage Brosman, "The Relativization of Character in *Les Faux-Monnayeurs*," *Modern Language Review*, 69 (1974), 777.
[57] Ibid., 774.   [58] Ibid., 771.

== II ==
Wieland:
Agathon (1767)*

Christoph Martin Wieland (1733-1813) is one of the most
remarkable figures of that period of a few decades
which saw the explosive emergence of German literature into full European status. He was a prolific writer,
and it is the measure of his bewildering creativity that
he was constantly capable of passionate literary en-
thusiasms, which he then outgrew. As a young man he
was influenced by pietism, and much of his early work
belongs to that ambience created by public enthusiasm
for Samuel Richardson and Friedrich Gottlieb Klop-
stock. Between 1762 and 1766 he published translations
of a number of Shakespeare's dramas. His versions may
not have worn well, but their very availability was important for the birth of the "Storm and Stress" (*Sturm
und Drang*), with its rapturous discovery of Shakespeare
as the true model for German literary talent to emulate.
Yet at this same time Wieland also made friends with
Graf Stadion, a great lover of French literature. In his
enthusiasm for classical and French models Wieland
evolved a characteristically urbane, light style both in
prose and verse. Most of his subsequent works bear
traces of a teasing rococo sensuality and a provocative
rationalism, which, however, are always tempered by
irony and playfulness. The most durable of his works
are *The Abderites* (1774), an engaging catalogue of the
systematic stupidities of the people of Abdera, and *Obe-
ron* (1780), a verse romance which brings a sophisticated

*This chapter is a reworked version of my paper, "An Unreadable
Novel? Some Observations on Wieland's *Agathon* and the Bildungsroman Tradition," *Publications of the English Goethe Society*, 45
(1975), 101ff. (hereafter cited as *PEGS*).

tongue-in-cheek narrative to bear on the fantastic medievalism of the subject matter. The text which concerns us here is his novel *Agathon*. In it, Wieland used his ironic sophistication to superb effect; indeed, irony is the source of the novel's extraordinary literary-historical importance.

For readers of English novels, *Agathon* might, I suspect, prove a somewhat forbidding prospect. It is a daunting novel, not just because of its length, but also because of its profuse digressions, digressions that are not mitigated by the exhilarating zaniness of, say, *Tristram Shandy*. We have an abundance of narrative commentary and discursive reflections on moral and epistemological questions that threatens to swamp the slender and not exactly gripping plot. Moreover, this wealth of narrative rumination is not only bulky, it is also curiously paradoxical and inconsistent. For this reason it can be nothing short of infuriating. One obvious example is the first few sentences of the Preface with which the novel opens: "The editor of this present story sees so little likelihood of persuading the public that it is in fact derived from an old Greek manuscript that he believes it is his best course of action to say nothing about this matter and to leave it up to the reader to think what he pleases" (375).[1] We begin, in other words, with a statement that is immediately withdrawn as pointless, which cannot but make us wonder why the statement should have been made in the first place. We may already suspect what in fact proves to be the case: the narrator does not abandon his references to the original manuscript, they recur frequently throughout the novel.

Having left the question of authenticity of source behind him, our narrator proceeds to raise the issue of

[1] References throughout are to Wieland, *Werke*, ed. F. Martini and H. Seiffert, I (Munich, 1964).

why we should be interested in such a person as
Agathon. It is suggested to us that the truth of any fictional work resides in its naturalness, in that it is con-
ceived in accordance with and shows respect for the
"ways of the world," that its characters "are not capriciously invented by the imagination or design of the author, but have been taken from the inexhaustible
storehouse of nature herself" (375). The human heart is
portrayed truthfully, naturally; the passions of which it
is capable are shown as arising from specific characteristics, from precisely documented circumstances.
Our narrator—or rather, "editor," as he continues to
designate himself despite the conclusion he has reached
in the opening paragraph—informs us that his chief aim
is to render the manifold nature of Agathon's being in
all its complexity, and that he has chosen this young
man to be his center of interest because of his intimate
acquaintance with the details of Agathon's life. He
blandly continues:

> For this reason he can reliably assert that Agathon
> and most of the other characters who are part of his
> story are real people. They are the sort of people
> who have existed in great numbers from time
> immemorial, and they exist to this very day.
> Moreover, he can say that—with the exception
> of some trifling circumstances, of certain conse-
> quences and specific details of chance events, and
> of whatever else belongs to the decorative embroid-
> ering of the story—everything that is essential to
> this story is as historically true and perhaps even a
> shade more authentic than anything written by the
> most reliable political historians which we at pres-
> ent possess. (376)

At this point the reader may be forgiven if his head
begins to spin slightly. Although we have already been
told that credibility in a work of art is not a question of

authenticated facts but of the reader's sense that the story could happen, we are now faced with special pleading to the effect that most of the characters had real-life originals. (*Most* of them, we ask ourselves, why not all?) We learn that some features of the story are not part of this authenticated reality. Well, which are they? Will we be able to distinguish them from the verifiable truth? And, to compound the confusion, we are told that the essence of the story is probably truer than anything written by the most scrupulous historians. It would seem, therefore, that the essential part will be essential whether it can be authenticated or not; indeed, it is the measure of its essentialness that it is more convincing than any verifiable facts. Of course, our narrator-editor continues, reality itself can be highly improbable (as even conscientious historians have attested), and for this reason "the author believes he has the right to expect that his readers will believe him absolutely when he positively asserts that Agathon did actually think or behave in a certain way" (376). Two comments seem to me appropriate here: first, the narrator, who has been the "editor" so far, now becomes the "author," which somewhat removes the note of special pleading for the authenticity of source material; second, at precisely the point when the "authenticity principle" seems to be on the wane we are most urgently requested to believe the writer when he strenuously asserts the factual accuracy of what he recounts.

The Preface concludes with some remarks on the character of Agathon himself. We are told that he is not a paragon of all the virtues, not a model of constancy and principle, and that this is the measure of his plausibility as a character. Moreover, we learn that our hero must be put to the test in the course of his journey through life and that only those readers who are themselves inclined to dishonesty and wickedness will be led astray by what they read (by the sophistry of Hippias,

for example). We are assured that it is the narrator's
plan that Agathon will learn from his various experiences, that he will end the novel as a wise and virtuous
man. All this sounds very admirable, even though such
assertions seem to contradict the early remarks to the effect that the truth (and value) of such a novel as this is to
be found in its naturalness, "that the characters are not
capriciously invented by the imagination or design of
the author" (375). We are now assured that there is a
"set of moral intentions which we have had in mind in
composing this work" (379).

I have summarized the arguments of the Preface in
such length and detail because the Preface quite clearly
establishes a whole set of narrative intimations which
are sustained throughout the novel.[2] Moreover, the
Preface initiates precisely that narrative discursiveness
of which I have spoken, a discursiveness that takes
many forms. There are a number of features of the novel
as a whole which I wish to highlight here. First, in the
debate about the nature and validity of the story the
reader is asked to bear in mind considerations of fictional truth and factual authenticity, of *Agathon* as a
novel and as an edited diary. Second, the reader finds
himself engaged in a debate about the nature of human
experience, about that human potentiality within himself which allows him to identify as valid and to identify
with fictional models of human behavior. Third, the
reader is engaged in a discussion about morals, about
the dialectic of general principles and specific cases, of
norms and the intractably individual, relative context to
which they must be related.[3] Fourth, the reader is in-
vited to reflect on human character, to ask to what ex-

[2] For an admirable analysis of the specifically aesthetic implications
of the Preface see Monika Schrader, *Mimesis und Poiesis* (Berlin and
New York, 1975), 95ff.

[3] For a full discussion of this aspect see A. Phelan, "The Nature and
Function of Irony in Five Major Novels of C. M. Wieland" (Ph.D.
diss., Cambridge University, 1974).

tent an intact, coherent self can be said to realize itself with a kind of cumulative consistency, and to what extent the personality is constantly in flux, a self-renewing complex of contradictory and compensatory energies and potentialities. These and other concerns are mediated through a carefully activated narrative field of reference: we have an original text and its modern fictive reworking, an original narrator and a present editor-cum-narrator, and, above all else, the reader as notional presence, apostrophized, cajoled, and buttonholed as part of the overall fiction.[4] Indeed, it is carefully suggested that there is a plurality of possible reader responses, and insofar as we are engaged in a debate with the narrator, we also find ourselves disputing our reading with notional fellow readers.

Two particular aspects of the complex of problems outlined above demand further consideration, largely because they highlight the interaction of discursive narrative fireworks and the overall import of the work. I have in mind the questions of Agathon's character and status as novel hero, and of the fiction of the original manuscript on which the novel is purportedly based. Obviously, the role and nature of Agathon is realized through the events that befall him. One might therefore begin by summarizing the plot of the novel. (I should make it clear here that I am concerned throughout with the first version of the novel, for reasons which I shall discuss later.) Agathon is a young man brought up in the orphic religion, a man concerned with the ideal existence which underlies all specific earthly forms. He loves, with a pure, sexless devotion, a young girl called Psyche, but is separated from her. For all that he is something of an idealist, a *Schwärmer*, Agathon changes tack when he has to leave Delphi. He is reunited with

---

[4] On the notion of the fictive reader see M. H. Würzner, "Die Figur des Lesers in Wielands *Geschichte des Agathon*," in *Dichter und Leser*, ed. F. van Ingen (Utrecht, 1972), 151ff.

his father and tries his hand at politics in Athens in an attempt to give palpable expression to his ideals of human conduct and society. But the populace is fickle; he is ousted from power and favor. He comes into the house of one Hippias, a sensualist who determines to make Agathon enjoy the pleasure of physical, particularly sexual, experience. Agathon meets and falls in love with Danae, a mature and beautiful woman who seduces him, not by any straightforward physical appeal, but by an inspired piece of playacting in which her body becomes the palpable enactment and realization of the image of Daphne. Agathon lives with Danae happily until he learns of her somewhat tempestuous sexual past, at which point he abandons her. He goes to Syracuse, again becomes involved in political activities, only to be disillusioned once more. Finally, he comes to Tarent, a community living under the wise government of Àrchytas. There he is reunited with Psyche—only to find that she is his sister. At the end of the novel he once again meets Danae, who has for some time been leading a secluded life in Archytas's land.

This very simple summary suggests the guiding principles behind Agathon's life. He is a man who oscillates between the active and the contemplative life, between public and private activity, between senses and spirit. He is a cluster of complementary energies: when he tries to be idealistic, he finds that the responses of his senses cloud his certainties; when he feels attracted toward Hippias and all he stands for, his idealism reasserts itself; when he is living a secluded life, he is attracted by politics; when he is in politics he feels the appeal of a life withdrawn from the turmoil of social living. At any given point in Agathon's story, we feel that there are more aspects to his personality than he is able to realize in any one pursuit or course of action. Moreover, he is not an unthinking person. Yet over and over again we sense that his self-examinations, his analyses of his situation, are too simple, are too much a flight into convenient labels and principles to do justice to the lability of his experiential capacities. Agathon is much less a known quantity, a manageable entity than any given activity, any given attempt at self-explication would suggest. So what is Agathon? In an attempt to deal with this question I shall look at one particularly crucial passage at the end of Book ix, Chapter 5. The narrator's invitation to his readers here to reflect on the persona of his hero is a concentrated example of the kinds of statements that are very much part of the narrator's running commentary throughout the novel.

Characteristically, the narrator begins, "We make a brief pause here, in order to give the reader time to consider what he at this point may have to say for or against our hero" (757). The primary issue, then, is how to evaluate Agathon's behavior. We have just learned that in a debating contest our hero has spoken out against the republican form of government; the narrator immediately suggests that in this context (as elsewhere) we must bear in mind that Agathon's views are of necessity affected by the specific experiences he has undergone (here, the ingratitude of the Athenians). He goes on to argue that those readers who uphold constancy of character and attitude as the supreme virtue must ask themselves whether this is not a totally unreal demand to make on a human being: given that everything around us changes, how should we be the one immovable, consistent entity? The narrator gives point to his general reflections by referring us to certain kinds of novel fiction: "In moral novels we do admittedly find heroes who remain true to themselves in everything—and who are to be praised for this. . . . But in life we find matters very different" (759). The criterion invoked is that of experience, of "life." It tells us that we only grow and develop by undertaking activities which change us, mislead us, and alienate us from ourselves: "We have already seen

our hero in various situations; and in each, through the
force of circumstance, a little different from what he really is" (759-60). Implicit here is the notion that the reality of Agathon is a complex, elusive self not fully expressed by any specific activity in which he is engaged.
The idea is clarified in the following passage: "He
seemed by turns [nach und nach] a pious idealist, a
platonist, a republican, a hero, a stoic, a voluptuary; and
he was none of these things, although he at various
times passed through all these phases and always a little
of each rubbed off on him. It will probably continue like
this for quite some time" (760). To observe the course of
Agathon's life up to this point is to observe a series of
events in linear sequence, a *Nacheinander*. Yet, potentially, he is all of those personae at one and the same
time; his self is a *Nebeneinander* which can never be
enacted in linear realization. The narrator is careful to
add a further point: it might be tempting to conclude
that this complex self can be apprehended as the sum
total of all his past actions, but this would be to presup-
pose that Agathon's life is over and done with, that he is
a known quantity to himself and to the readers, that
there is no room for further change, for further activation of potential selves. The narrator advises caution
here: what Agathon has been up to the present is not an
exhaustive living out of his potentiality. Rather, his self
is the result of chance; a contingent sequence of occur-
rences has activated him to various kinds of response.
We must not judge prematurely, because we cannot
claim premature certainty about him:

> But of his character, of what he really was and of
> what remained constant about him under all these
> disguises . . . of all this we cannot yet speak. Hence,
> without passing premature judgment—a thing we
> are accustomed to do time and time again in every-
> day life—we will continue to observe him . . . and

to refrain from evaluating the totality of his moral
being until such time as we are acquainted with it.
(760)

Interestingly, the narrator here reverses the emphasis in
the comparison between literature (the novel) and life.
In our everyday experience we are forced by pragmatic
considerations into premature judgments (both epistemological and moral). But in terms of our interpretative relationship to this novel fiction before us, we can
afford the luxury of scrupulousness, we can admit to
complexities, to the vital dimension of that which has
not yet become reality, of futurity as an abiding factor
which must condition our response to a human being.
Thus the narrator dismantles whatever clarity we think
we may have attained about the protagonist (or indeed,
whatever clarity the protagonist may think he has
achieved about himself). The security of our cognitive
and evaluative relationship to Agathon's character is
disturbed by a two-pronged attack which criticizes a certain kind of novel fiction for its crude model of human
behavior, and which also criticizes the realm of everyday human interaction for its adherence to simplistic,
pragmatic judgments.

The implications of these narrative reflections are
many and complex. Most obviously, they would appear
to call into question any straightforward, cumulatively
linear teleology in the novel. One begins to wonder
whether there will ever be a watershed in Agathon's life
from which point on we will know him reliably, fully,
consistently. We also wonder whether Agathon himself
will ever achieve such clarity, whether there is a set of
insights which can be possessed once and for all.
Moreover, one wonders whether such perfect cognition
would automatically entail a particular kind of practical
behavior (a certain career or activity). The import of the
narrator's running commentary serves to suggest that

such certainty is impossible because it could only be attained as a kind of Archimedean point located outside the self, outside the context of its living and functioning. And yet, in total disregard of such considerations, our narrator at times writes with a kind of sovereign assurance—both epistemological and moral—which seems to make nonsense of his earlier statements. One can, for example, find passages of evaluative commentary which seem curiously simplistic. This is particularly noticeable in the narrator's treatment of the Agathon-Danae relationship. At times he shows himself fully able to suggest the complexity of what is involved here, the process of mutual enrichment and transformation, the volatile interplay of reality and erotic illusion.[5] At other times, however, he manifests a curious censoriousness and unproblematic, even self-righteous, certainty. For example, he describes Agathon and Danae as being "happy in this sweet infatuation" (525) and later insists that Agathon's involvement with Danae is a kind of aberration, "a lengthy progression along those mistaken paths on to which he had strayed" (534). Particularly significant is the end of Book vii, Chapter 9, where Agathon abandons Danae: "But as soon as it had come to the point where he believed himself deceived in his opinion of her character and moral worth, as soon as he found himself compelled to despise her—then she ceased to be Danae for him. And by a completely natural sequence of events, he again became Agathon in that same moment" (636). Of course, there is an element of doubt inherent in these remarks (one notes that Agathon *believes* himself to have been deceived), but even so, the statement betrays a certainty about the hero's selfhood which is in marked contradistinction to the narrator's tentativeness about the nature of his pro-

---

[5] See Kurt Wölfel, "Daphnes Verwandlungen: Zu einem Kapitel in Wielands *Agathon*," *Jahrbuch der deutschen Schillergesellschaft*, 8 (1964), 41ff.

tagonist. In part, such a certainty is shared by Agathon himself. When he set off for Syracuse, "he felt again that he was Agathon" (670). Later, when Agathon is overcome with longing for his pure, beloved Psyche, the narrator affirms that "all these symptoms vouch for the fact that he is still Agathon" (826). Such remarks set up a sustained implication that there *is* a known quantity Agathon, a constant individual whose life grows with necessity and coherence out of that childhood self raised in the temple environment. And that constant self would appear to be none other than Agathon the idealist, the *Schwärmer*. The reasons for this curiously disingenuous view of the main character are, in my view, bound up with the whole fiction of the original manuscript, to which I shall return.

I have already referred to the fact that the debate about character is channeled through a debate about novel fiction, about the reader's response to this present story and to other kinds of novels he has met. Part of the narrator's constant barrage of criticism is mounted against those who always know how to interpret a situation, how to evaluate a character. The narrator's long-windedness and all-pervading uncertainty become crystallized in his frequent assertions of the unnovellike quality of his intrusiveness. Indeed, he is prepared on occasion to suggest that the alienated reader who finds such digressions inappropriate in a novel may wish to skip the discursive interludes. *Agathon* is, then, a novel which makes traditional novel fiction (and its attendant expectations) explicitly thematic and challenges them. One might almost say that it is a novel which proclaims itself unreadable by the criteria of the traditional novel—but goes on to ask whether the traditional novel is worth reading in the first place.[6] Particularly signifi-

---

[6] For an admirable discussion of this regeneration of the novel convention see Fritz Martini's "Nachwort" in Wieland, *Werke*, I, 945. See also Klaus Oettinger, *Phantasie und Erfahrung: Studien zur Erzählpoetik C. M. Wielands* (Munich, 1970), 86ff.

cant is the passage where we are explicitly told that Agathon is not really a novel hero:

> What we are essentially after with these remarks is simply that the kind of novel heroes we have been talking about are even less to be found within the realm of nature than are lions with wings or fish with girls' bodies . . . and that therefore the hero of our story, as a result of the changes and weaknesses to which we have seen him prone, is of course—we admit it—less of a hero, but the more so is he a man. And the more is he able to instruct us by his experience—even by his faults. (513)

It is the measure of the human probability of the figure of Agathon that he is precisely *not* a traditional novel hero, that morally and psychologically he is not a constant.

This brings me to a final point about narration in this novel: the constant references to the original manuscript. Here, of course, we are confronted by an ironic tension of assertions and intimations. On the one hand, we are asked to believe that the original manuscript is based on Agathon's own account of his life; hence it is authentic, and therefore, unchangeable. On the other hand, we are made clearly aware that the original manuscript reports a wildly providential story. Our narrator is able to use this story as a cipher for a mode of unsophisticated narration, for unsophisticated portrayal of the self as a known quantity—and can criticize it in terms of his own (modern) awareness of psychological (and hence, narrative) complexity. The opening of Chapter 5 of Book x is a sustained example of what I mean: "The author of the old manuscript from which we admit to having taken the greater part of this story, is, as we have seen, triumphant because he has managed to get his hero away from a court with his virtue entirely intact" (811-12). But this is followed by an enormous digression on the nature of human virtue and integrity. It concludes: "Our thoughtful readers will quite clearly understand why we have scruples about applauding the original author of the Greek manuscript in his all too favorable assessment of the present moral state of our hero" (823-24). The suggestion is, of course, that we as modern readers have to be infinitely more cautious in our judgments than was the original writer.

The ironic fiction of the original manuscript allows Wieland to have his cake and eat it. But one still wonders why he should have bothered to incorporate this further strand of narrative intimation into his novel. The observations about verisimilitude and authenticity, about the complexity of modern reader responses vis-à-vis narratively naive fictional modes, have already been made with sufficient thoroughness. One must ask quite simply why Wieland bothered with the fiction of the original manuscript. There is, I think, one significant answer which is part and parcel of the whole problem of character and plot with which I have been concerned. The particular function I have in mind asserts itself with greatest clarity toward the end of the novel. Book XI begins with a criticism of the original author for having betrayed all concern for verisimilitude in order to furnish his readers with a resounding happy ending to the story: "In this, the eleventh, book, we must admit that our author appears to have strayed somewhat from this our world . . . into the land of ideas, of miracles, of events which turn out exactly as one might have wished, into, to say it all over again, the land of Beautiful Souls and utopian republics" (827).[7] It would appear that the temptation has proved too great: the original author decided "to test and cleanse his [Agathon's] virtue, and to bring it to the required consistency" (828), so

[7] For a discussion of this point in *Agathon* and other Bildungsromane see Gerda Röder, *Glück und glückliches Ende im deutschen Bildungsroman* (Munich, 1968).

that the novel could end with a worthily climactic conclusion. This narrative teleology strikes the narrator
(and his readers) as patently improbable, "but what is a
poor author to do?" (831). The author's solution resides
in a further polarization of the irony: the original manuscript is scrupulously adhered to but is called relentlessly into question at every turn. Indeed, our narrator
goes so far as to turn this critical method on himself:

> The intentions which led him to publish the old
> manuscript, which came into his hands by chance,
> in a version whose form and character has been
> sufficiently illustrated by the previous ten books,
> have already been fulfilled. It is, we trust, unneces-
> sary that we go into greater detail here. Yet this
> much we can say: that we have never intended to
> write a novel—although many may not have got
> this into their heads despite the title and the
> preface—and as this book, insofar as the editor has
> had a hand in it, is no novel, nor is intended to be
> one, he, the editor, can summon up little interest in
> the so-called tying of the knot—in the question
> whether the author of the manuscript has un-
> raveled or cut the knot skillfully or clumsily. (831)

Despite all appearances to the contrary (appearances,
we should add, which the narrator has most carefully
exploited), the book we have been reading is apparently
no novel. For this reason it does not matter whether the
original has a felicitous or awkward conclusion: either
way, it remains "novel material," and our narrator has
so far distanced himself from such fictions that any tin-
kering with the original would be utterly superfluous.
Book XI is, accordingly, allowed to proceed on its triumphant way as it chronicles the reunion of Agathon,
Psyche, and Danae. "And why not?" asks the narrator,
"now that we all know how happy we can make our
friend Agathon in the process" (845). Psyche, we are

told, has been saved from the hands of pirates by a storm, and the narrator adds a heavily ironic defense of the stock-in-trade of the providential novel ending: "You really have no cause to complain, gentlemen, for it is, to the best of our knowledge, the first storm in this story" (846).

The concluding book of the novel reveals the full import of Wieland's irony, the extent to which he enabled himself to have his cake and eat it. At one level, novel convention is serenely allowed to take its course—because, one is tempted to add, Wieland would otherwise have denied himself the possibility of ending the enterprise on which he had embarked. In other words, he can both mount a critique of the novel genre and tell a novel at the same time. But this is not to be seen simply as some kind of urbane in-joke with the reader. For the discussion of novel expectations, of expectations about plot and character, is the principal channel by which Wieland brings into focus a much larger debate about issues of human cognition and value judgments, about moral norms and principles, about epistemological certainties. In order to initiate and to sustain this debate, Wieland had to intimate not only critique, but also the object of his critique. That is, he had to bounce his questioning off the stability and the simplistic human and narrative *donnée* of the traditional novel form. Without that ironic undertaking, without that "critical-analytical relationship to the narratable,"[8] without that obstinate remnant of traditional novel plot, Wieland's *Agathon* would cease to be a work of narrative fiction. At that point, of course, one asks why Wieland should have wished to write any kind of novel in the first place.

---

[8] W. Preisendanz, "Die Auseinandersetzung mit dem Nachahmungsprinzip in Deutschland und die besondere Rolle der Romane Wielands," in *Nachahmung und Illusion*, ed. H. R. Jauss (Munich, 1964), 128. See also Wolfgang Iser's discussion of the eighteenth-century English novel in *Der Implizite Leser* (Munich, 1972), 13ff.

Why should he not have written some kind of philosophical or epistemological tract? Why did he not have
the strength of his discursive convictions, of his *Es-*
sayismus, avant la lettre? The answer must surely
be—and this is the profoundest legitimation of the
ironic stance adopted in *Agathon*—that there is an essential truth about even the most rudimentary of novel fictions. However much human character, for example,
may be infinitely more complex than the traditional
novel allows, may be a vitally interacting *Nebeneinander*,
yet man, whether he likes it or not, does live and move
within the *Nacheinander* of linear time. His life does have
a plot, and, in part at least, he must conceive of himself
in terms of a kind of personal and general historicity if
he is to have any workable sense of his own identity, of
those activities which are more rather than less appropriate to that self. Hence the narrator's curiously simplistic comments about Agathon as a character. They
have a legitimate role to play in the whole debate about
the protagonist's character because they are one pole of
the dialectic which informs the novel. They constitute
the stability which defines the volatility and flux of
Agathon's character.

In one sense, the truth about Agathon is unknowable,
is more than he can realize (in both senses of the word)
at any one time. In another sense, he does have a story,
a sequence of experiences which are inalienably his.
And if he has a story, then the novel can have a plot. But
the story is only part of the truth. Wieland's difficulties
about concluding his story were real enough, as he revealed in a letter of July 1766: "What do you say to
Agathon? How do you believe it will end? And how
would you like it to end? Be so kind and give me a fairly
detailed answer: you can take as much time as you
need."[9] This could be the narrator addressing his

[9] *Ausgewählte Briefe von C. M. Wieland*, II (Zurich, 1815), 268.

readers. The difficulty about ending the novel was not artistic incapacity on Wieland's part but grew of necessity from his perception of human and fictional affairs. Because of the intractability of the problem, the first version of *Agathon* has an ending which the narrator relentlessly calls into question. Friedrich Sengle is surely right to stress that this first version has "the truth of the fragment,"[10] an argument reinforced by Fritz Martini: "in its fragmentary character resided the personal and historical truthfulness of this book."[11] For this reason I have devoted my attention throughout this chapter to the first version of *Agathon* and not to those subsequent editions in which Wieland strove increasingly to round off the novel. The truth of the conclusion to the first version is that it shows how at one level and within one set of terms Agathon's life so far can be brought to a conclusion, while at another level and within another set of terms his life cannot possibly be declared, even provisionally, closed.

Agathon is a difficult novel, but it is surely one that speaks with particular urgency to modern readers. We are, after all, used to reading novels about the impossibility (or, more accurately, the inauthenticity) of writing traditional novels. But such considerations are not the exclusive preserve of the twentieth-century novel. It is noteworthy that in a recent book on novel theory Gerhart von Graevenitz insists that many novels operate with a kind of "essayism" whereby they relativize their own referential intactness as texts.[12] And it is hardly surprising that the examples he uses to illustrate his thesis are such works as *Wilhelm Meister's Apprenticeship*, *Indian Summer*, and *The Magic Mountain*, novels

[10] Sengle, *Wieland* (Stuttgart, 1949), 196.
[11] Martini, "Nachwort," in Wieland, *Werke*, i, 941.
[12] Graevenitz, *Die Setzung des Subjekts* (Tübingen, 1973).

which critical consensus has so often dubbed Bildungsromane. If I may allow myself a polemical formulation, *Agathon* achieves its modernity because of, not in spite of, its historical significance as the first of the great Bildungsromane.

═ III ═

Goethe:
Wilhelm Meister's Apprenticeship
(1795-1796)

Wilhelm Meister, a young man of bourgeois background, has since childhood been fascinated by the theater. So we learn from the beginning of Goethe's novel.
As the story opens, we discover that the adolescent
Wilhelm's enthusiasm is compounded by a further infatuation: he is desperately in love with a young actress
called Marianne, but he is subsequently persuaded to
break the relationship when he observes her, as he
thinks, being unfaithful to him. This bitter blow is not
the end of Wilhelm's involvement with the theater,
however. A business trip undertaken on his father's be-
half brings him into contact with a group of actors, and
he puts up the money to establish the troupe as a going
concern. After many vicissitudes, Wilhelm and his fellow actors join Serlo's famous theatrical company. This
new collaboration bears fruit in a production of *Hamlet*,
but Wilhelm gradually becomes estranged from the
world of the theater. Book VI of the novel consists of an
interpolated diary, the "Confessions of a Beautiful
Soul," which catalogues a woman's growth to certainty
of purpose and spiritual self-fulfillment. In one sense,
the interpolated manuscript is only tenuously con-
nected with the plot of the novel (the "beautiful soul" is
the aunt of Natalie, whom Wilhelm marries at the end of
the novel). But in a thematic sense, the diary has an important transitional function: Wilhelm's involvement
with the theater has in a variety of ways made possible
an exploration and broadening of his personality. The

theater has offered an adventurous, nomadic existence, the chance to extend the self through the adoption of various roles, but it is an existence without cohesion and focus. The diary shows us and our hero how one human being finds fulfillment by withdrawal from the world, by a life of concentrated inwardness. The second section of the novel (after the "Confessions") shows us how Wilhelm gradually moves away from the theater, how he becomes increasingly drawn to an aristocratic world which has its center and controlling purpose in a secret society, the so-called Society of the Tower. Wilhelm is admitted to this society, and, after much error and uncertainty, finally finds true fulfillment in marrying Natalie, the sister of Lothario, one of the most energetic and forceful members of the Society of the Tower.

Such, in bare outline, is the event sequence of Goethe's novel. The plot is a curious one, for it is an unsettling mixture of the episodic and the providential. It is episodic in the sense that Wilhelm wanders through experience without gaining any precise sense of where he is going, of what he is achieving in the process. Yet, countermanding this episodic feel are numerous indications that there is purpose to the randomness, that there is cohesion, order, and pattern to the seeming aimlessness and fortuitousness of the life chronicled.[1] On several occasions Wilhelm receives advice in the form of mysterious intimations from unknown figures who are apparently watching over him. At times, Wilhelm himself feels that a fresh meeting, a new encounter, is somehow *not* new, that it has been prepared for. When he is attracted to the Countess, he is (without knowing it) attracted to Natalie's sister, and hence to a prefiguration of his destined partner. Moreover, later in the novel Wilhelm glimpses Natalie as a beautiful Amazon who

[1] For an admirable discussion of the providentiality of the plot see Hans Eichner, "Zur Deutung von *Wilhelm Meisters Lehrjahren*," *Jahrbuch des freien deutschen Hochstifts* (Frankfurt, 1966), 182ff.

succours him and his friends after they have been at-
tacked and robbed. He loses sight of her but never
forgets her image. That image of the Amazon is
nourished by an image that was very much part of his
childhood: a painting of the ailing son of a king being
comforted by a beautiful, sympathetic woman.[2] When
Natalie helps Wilhelm and his fellows, the surprise appearance of a beautiful, enigmatic woman is given a resonance that links it inalienably to something embedded
in the hero's selfhood. Furthermore, as Wilhelm comes
to know Natalie later in the novel, he will discover in
her house all the *objets d'art* which his grandfather had
collected and which in his early years had meant a great
deal to him.

In addition to such links, more obvious recurrences of
character coalesce to form an ongoing providentiality
within the plot sequence.[3] This providentiality is two-
edged in that it allows characters both to reappear and
to fade in a remarkably convenient way. Hence,
Marianne, Aurelie, and Lydia (and ultimately Mignon
and the Harper as well) can be, as it were, written out of
the novel when the need arises, whereas Natalie
emerges as part of a whole web of links and relationships (she is the sister of the Countess, Friedrich, and
Lothario, and the niece of the Beautiful Soul). Indeed,
the world through which Wilhelm moves takes a very
beneficent interest in regulating his life. Wilhelm is pre-
vented from marrying Therese by the fortunate timing
of her discovery that she is in fact able to marry
Lothario. Wilhelm is thus shielded from the consequences of a wrong decision. This gives the sense that

---

[2] As David Roberts suggests, the picture of the ailing prince who is
in love with his father's bride also prefigures Wilhelm's involvement
with *Hamlet*. See "Wilhelm Meister and Hamlet," *PEGS*, 45 (1975), 66.

[3] For a discussion of the sociological implications of this ongoing
providentiality, and of its links with bourgeois-liberal economic
theory, see Stefan Blessin, "Die radikal-liberale Konzeption von
Wilhelm Meisters Lehrjahren," *DVLG*, 49 (1975), 190*-225*.

Wilhelm's life, for all its adventurousness and wandering, is curiously sheltered and protected. The possibility of error is always given of course, but with no sense of irredeemability. As a result, the plot lacks a certain bite: there is little finality, little once-and-for-all linearity to Wilhelm's experiences. This quality informs even the narrative. A good deal of irony accompanies the explicit depictions of the error, self-deception, and confusion inherent in Wilhelm's frequent attempts to understand himself and his needs. Yet the irony is never doom-laden; it never implies incorrigibility and disaster. Indeed, the narrator frequently adopts a generalizing perspective; by employing such pronouns as "we" or "one" he asks for our conciliatory assent to the human capacity for error. The attendant perspective of hindsight and detachment intimates that error will not have the last word.

Such is the curiously half-hearted relationship of Wilhelm to his experience, and this privileged tentativeness within the living process makes the plot less than full-blooded or gripping. What is particularly intriguing is that the tentativeness is maintained right through to the closing pages. The beneficently stage-managed reality through which Wilhelm moves would seem to promise a more resoundingly happy ending than Goethe in fact provides. Indeed, a reader might find it embarrassingly difficult to describe with any certainty or precision just what goal Wilhelm attains in the course of the novel. Clearly, there are two centers to Wilhelm's involvement with the world around him, the theater and the Society of the Tower. An examination of both spheres of being and activity can help us toward an understanding of Wilhelm's development.

I have already suggested that the theater appeals to Wilhelm because it promises a fuller extension of the human personality than anything vouchsafed by bourgeois existence. The essence of the theater is the

physical, palpable enactment of an illusion. In this sense
it is a place where the actor can transform a fictive possibility into a circumscribed reality. As Wilhelm tries to
explain to his bourgeois friend Werner in Book II, Chapter 2, art in general (and the theater in particular, we
may add) is an answer to the dissatisfactions that
man feels within the narrow confines of practical social
reality:

> What is it that keeps men in continual discontent
> and agitation? It is that they cannot make realities
> correspond with their conceptions, that enjoyment
> steals away from among their hands, that the
> wished-for comes too late, and nothing reached
> and acquired produces on the heart the effect which
> their longing for it at a distance led them to an-
> ticipate. Now fate has exalted the poet above all
> this. . . . (82-83)[4]

Art, then, is a realm in which the real and the possible,
the finite and the infinite, meet and interlock. In this
sense, as becomes clear in Wilhelm's wonderment at the
Hall of the Past, art can allow man a glimpse of a totality
and coherence that his everyday experience never provides. For this reason artistic impressions consistently
provide crystallization points in Wilhelm's quest for
self-knowledge. Moreover, the theater is a specifically
social art; it depends on a corporate identity. In Book II,
Chapter 4, Wilhelm advocates the theater as an agency
for social cohesion, as an art that has direct bearing on
society: "We have a lively proof how useful the theater
might be to all ranks; what advantage even the state
might procure from it, if the occupations, trades, and
undertakings of men were brought upon the stage and
presented on their praiseworthy side" (95). Like the

---

[4] References throughout are to the *Hamburger Ausgabe*, VII. My
translations draw extensively on Thomas Carlyle's version.

songs of the Harper and Mignon, the theater opens up
in Wilhelm a world of imagination which is all too often
denied validity in the practical world. At the same time,
the theater, particularly popular theater, has a tingling,
almost erotic appeal and immediacy. This quality is possessed in large measure by Philine and her songs.
Wilhelm looks forward to a situation in which the sensuous appeal of the popular theater could be married
with intellectual and moral seriousness, with the result
that the idea could truly be made flesh:

> What actor, what author, nay, what man of any
> class, would not regard himself as on the summit of
> his wishes, could he, by a noble saying or worthy
> action, produce so universal an impression? What a
> precious emotion would it give, if one could dis-
> seminate generous, exalted, manly feelings with
> electric force and speed, and rouse assembled
> thousands into rapture, as these people [the tum-
> blers] by their bodily alertness have done! (106)

Wilhelm's wish-dream here takes up one of the major
themes of the novel: the relationship between reality
and idea, between activity and reflection.

Other aspects of Wilhelm's involvement with the theater also have an unmistakable thematic import. One is
the relationship of parts and whole. Over and over
again, in Wilhelm's discussion of plays and in his own
attempts at writing, we are made to see the hero's immaturity as an inability to grasp the whole process of
human living. His early efforts at playwriting tend to be
all heroes and soliloquies and no action. Drama must
involve a total process of human interaction, one in
which the grand soliloquies, the high points of reflection and self-exploration, are yet seen to be embedded
in a chain of specific political, social, and psychological
causality. The vital focus for this whole debate in
Goethe's novel is to be found in the many discussions of

Hamlet. As Wilhelm wrestles with Shakespeare's play, he is forced to reflect not simply on the practicalities of theatrical production, but on certain philosophical problems, on a figure whose relationship to the world around him is troubled to the point of dislocation, and on the total emotional and social situation of which Hamlet's life (and thinking) is a part. At times Wilhelm's enthusiasm for the play amounts to virtual identification with its protagonist, at times he feels impelled to cut and rewrite Shakespeare's text. The hero's involvement with *Hamlet* is anything but a gratuitously discursive exercise in Shakespeare criticism; rather, it engages Wilhelm both imaginatively and practically, both intellectually and emotionally. Wilhelm is, vis-à-vis *Hamlet*, actor, producer, writer, and critic. Goethe is able to suggest, with masterly skill, the excitement of self-discovery in Wilhelm's relationship to *Hamlet*—and the hero's continuing limitations and inadequacies.

Wilhelm's love affair with the theater is, then, profoundly important, but it does not leave him in obvious and unassailable possession of a certain wisdom or insight which we (let alone he) can formulate discursively. Nor does the theater prove to be his destined sphere of practical activity. His abandonment of the theater comes gradually as a kind of organic process of "growing out" of the theater. There are no obvious epiphanies or turning points. Goethe is careful to maintain the interrelationship between Wilhelm's theatrical experiences and his capacities as a human being. Nonetheless, he suggests at the same time that there need be no obvious one-to-one correlation between the two spheres. In one sense, playing a role in the theater is like playing a role in life; in another sense, the two worlds are distinct, the chameleonlike existence of the actor being almost a disqualification from practical living. Serlo's irresponsibility is what makes him the superb performer he is. On the other hand, it would be wrong to conclude that

Wilhelm's attachment to the theater is simply an aberration which he must cast aside as soon as possible in favor of a firm commitment to practical living. Even through all his disappointments, Wilhelm retains an obscure sense that the theater can teach him about life and that life can deepen his insight into the theater. The description of Wilhelm's decision to accompany the actors to the castle sounds promising: "Wilhelm, who had come from home to study men, was unwilling to let slip this opportunity of examining the great world, where he expected to obtain much insight into life, into himself, and the dramatic art" (154). Yet the Wilhelm whose fortunes we follow hardly seems to be involved in an unequivocal development toward maturity. Aurelie at one point comments on the discrepancy between Wilhelm's growing sophistication in aesthetic matters and his immovable naivety in human affairs: "Hearing you expound the mysteries of Shakespeare, one would think you had just descended from a synod of the gods, and had listened there while they were taking counsel how to form men; in seeing you transact with your fellows, I could imagine you to be the first large-born child of the Creation" (257).

Goethe, in fact, is remarkably oblique in his treatment of Wilhelm's development. And this is particularly tantalizing, since the reader expects some clear intimation as to what he should make of Wilhelm's theatrical progress. On the other hand, there is a refreshing astringency to Goethe's obliqueness: he refuses to take the easy way out, to document sustained linear progression toward a goal. Instead, he continues to insist that the hero's life is simply more unfocused than this. It is significant that Wilhelm, in a late interview with Werner, does assert that he has learned something from his involvement with the theater: he has discovered that in the theater, even the privileged onlooker does not know what to make of the lives put before him. Moreover, in actual dealings with people, man can be even less sure in his judgments because he is part of the process he is trying to interpret: "How can men judge rightly of our actions, which appear but singly or in fragments to them. . . . Are not actors and actresses in a play set up on boards before them; lamps are lit on every side; the whole transaction is comprised within three hours; yet scarcely one of them knows rightly what to make of it" (500). One is tempted to add that Goethe's novel, too, denies us the ability to "know rightly what to make of it." And, maddeningly, this is true even of the second section of the novel, in which Wilhelm is admitted to the Society of the Tower. Here we have a highly structured world, sustained by maxims and ideas, by discursively formulated aims and principles. There is no shortage of pedagogues eager to debate with Wilhelm. After the confused turmoil of our hero's theatrical wanderings, it is a relief to enter a realm of ideas and values, except that, even here, our hero's experience obstinately refuses to yield interpretative clarity. It is almost as though Goethe were deliberately playing with reader expectations—the novel of the secret society was very much part of the popular taste of the time—but only in order to channel these expectations into the service of his own much more complex undertaking.[5]

The Society of the Tower is a secret society made up chiefly of aristocrats whose avowed concern is both with the growth and unfolding of individual human capacities and with that interaction of specific talents and temperaments which yields the totality of human society. The central ideas are discussed in Book VIII, Chapter 5, where Jarno speaks of the early days of the society:

---

[5] For a discussion of Goethe's "borrowing" see M. Thalmann, *Der Trivialroman des 18. Jahrhunderts und der romantische Roman* (Berlin, 1923), M. Beaujean, *Der Trivialroman in der zweiten Hälfte des 18. Jahrhunderts* (Bonn, 1964), and H. Emmel, *Was Goethe vom Roman der Zeitgenossen nahm* (Bern, 1972).

"We began to see nothing but the errors and narrowness of others, and to think of ourselves as superior beings. The Abbé came to our aid and taught us that one should not observe one's fellow men without at the same time concerning oneself with their improvement [Bildung]" (549). The society, with all its rites and observances, is devoted to human growth and self-improvement. But it is not simply a protected enclave, a kind of boarding school; rather, it is a reference point for active lives. The Abbé insists very firmly that "man is only able to watch and eavesdrop on himself when he is active" (549). But on the other hand, the Society of the Tower seems to represent a very definite goal to be attained: admission to its membership marks a stage in an individual's life (all its members contribute the history of their apprenticeships, their *Lehrjahre*, to an archive). Its graduates, we learn, are people "who felt strongly and who clearly affirmed that which they were born to be" (549-50). Self-knowledge appears to be the vital criterion for making this affirmation, and self-knowledge in its turn entails a willing and knowing acceptance of what one is destined to be, of one's limitation to a given selfhood, and of the practical activity appropriate to that selfhood. Oddly enough, however, our hero does not seem to be in possession of such certainty of purpose.

The Abbé is the vital focus of the Society of the Tower. He recognizes and affirms the specificity of the individual in all his particular (that is, limited) gifts and capacities, yet at the same time he is able to perceive and value the whole of which these individuals are part. Thereby the Abbé constantly supplies the corrective of wholeness to the specificity of individual lives. He possesses the "overview . . . over all the energies which dwell in man and of which each can be developed according to its kind" (552). He is the necessary center from which the individual life is rounded out to perfect complementariness with other lives: "Most men—even the most excellent of them—are limited. . . . Each one values certain qualities in himself and in other people; these are the only ones he favors, these are the only ones he wants to see developed" (552). The Abbé pulls in the opposite direction: he has reverence for the wholeness of human potential in mankind. He respects the simplest handicraft and the most sophisticated art, the babbling of the child and the rhetoric of the singer, gentle sympathy and blazing passion, sensuous immediacy and insubstantial intimation. All these capacities must be furthered, but among the *generality* of a human society: "all that and much more is present in man and must be developed: but not in one, rather in many" (552). Thus the wholeness of humanity is to be realized in the corporate realm of society. What can only be a potentiality in one man is realized in the practical activity of another.[6] Within the society itself, Lothario, the man of boundless energy, grandiose plans, and long-term vision, is counterbalanced by the doctor, who sees above all *present* needs and circumstances. This is the central conception of the Society of the Tower, a vision of human totality which reconciles the necessary limitation of the self to one sphere of practical being and activity with the wholeness that slumbers as a clustering of potentiality in each man. Such is Goethe's answer to the growing dangers of the compartmentalization and specialization he perceived in the society around him. What he attempted was the reconciliation of limitation and totality, of practical activity and human potential, of (in Hegel's terms) the prose of the workaday world and the poetry of the individual heart and imagination.[7]

The manifest weight and seriousness attributed to the

[6] Eichner discusses the limitations of the various members of the Society of the Tower—Jarno's coldness, Lothario's ruthlessness, Natalie's saintliness (bought at the price of sacrificing vitality and passion). See his "Zur Deutung von *Wilhelm Meisters Lehrjahren*," 183ff. See also G. Storz, "Wieder einmal die *Lehrjahre*," in *Versuche zu Goethe* (*Festschrift für E. Heller*), ed. V. Dürr and G. von Molnár (Heidelberg, 1976), esp. 198-99.

[7] See V. Lange, "Goethe's Craft of Fiction," *PEGS*, 22 (1952-53), 31ff.

ideas behind the Society of the Tower makes it tempting to assume that the society is the goal of Wilhelm's quest. Yet Wilhelm's behavior after his admission to the society hardly allows us to be confident that he has developed in any clear-cut way. The events that befall him of course look decisive: he undergoes an initiation ceremony of much ritual and splendor, during which he is presented with a scroll containing all manner of maxims and wise teachings; he is confirmed in the knowledge that Felix is indeed his son. And the Abbé pronounces words of benediction and graduation over him: "Hail to thee, young man. Thy apprenticeship is done: Nature has pronounced thee free" (497). This looks like the final achievement of wisdom, and one cannot help but think that the novel as a whole would have a much more unequivocal feel if it ended here (perhaps with a final sentence in which Wilhelm is joined with Natalie, his destined partner). But the novel does not end here. Wilhelm feels that he can see his way clear. He decides that Therese is the appropriate wife for himself (and mother for Felix), and he accordingly, with a sense of purposive clarity altogether rare in his experience so far, writes a letter proposing marriage to her. Yet this very action, seemingly the product of new-found mastery, proves to be yet another error. Wilhelm's decision is not, apparently, the full and balanced wisdom of the whole man: it is an excessively cerebral proceeding which ignores his deepest needs and affections (which are centered on Natalie, the "Beautiful Amazon"). From the consequences of this error Wilhelm is delivered by the fortunate discovery that Therese is after all able to marry Lothario. Before a happy ending can be brought about, however, Wilhelm goes through much anguish and heart-searching. His despair issues in a resentment of the seeming finality of his admission to the Society of the Tower. He feels, as he expresses to Jarno, that expectations of once-and-for-all mastery have been im-

planted in him, but that the reality of his capacities lags
far behind:

> We are led with great solemnity to a place which
> truly inspires awe, we are allowed to see the most
> wondrous visions, we are given scrolls full of mar-
> vellous, secret sayings—of which we admittedly
> understand but the smallest part—we are informed
> that up to now we were apprentices, we are pro-
> nounced ready and allowed to go, and we are no
> wiser than before. (548)

Wilhelm's exasperation results from the divided perception that he has both reached and not reached some significant turning point in his life. He is left feeling unenlightened, and the richer, by the few maxims which he
holds in his hand. Indeed, as Karl Schlechta points out
with great urgency,[8] there is undeniably something sententious and petrified about the Society of the Tower.
When Wilhelm is explaining his difficulties to Jarno, the
latter even has recourse to Wilhelm's scroll for a handy
maxim: " 'I must just have a quick glance at the scroll!'
Jarno continued, 'all men constitute the world' " (552).
Later Wilhelm will express his resentment at this
schoolmasterly fondness for precepts and wise sayings.
He even interrupts Jarno with the exclamation, "For
Heaven's sake, no more maxims!" (553). On one level,
Wilhelm's irritation is the result of personal feelings of
inadequacy and resentment. Yet, on another level, he
expresses a valid criticism of the Society of the Tower.
For he perceives the wordiness, the excessive discur-
siveness of this secret club built to human wholeness.[9]

There is, then, an implied reservation about the Society of the Tower, a refusal on Goethe's part to make it
the goal of Wilhelm's life—all of which contributes to

[8] Schlechta, *Goethes Wilhelm Meister* (Frankfurt, 1953), 64ff.
[9] See Blackall's judicious discussion of the Society of the Tower in
Goethe and the Novel (Ithaca and London, 1976), 301-2.

the obliqueness of the novel. (It is worth remembering that Goethe himself was reluctant to strengthen the thesis or central idea of his novel: he expressed dislike for "any clear-cut message which appeals to the conceptual faculty alone.")[10] In other words, the novel suggests that human wholeness is something that cannot be possessed in the serene acquirement of specific lessons or insights. It is, rather, a clustering of potentialities, an intimation of the possible, which the individual carries with him as he lives his life. When Jarno says that "there are few who at once have Thought and the capacity for Action: Thought expands, but lames; Action animates but narrows" (550), he expresses the central tension in the novel which unites both the theatrical episodes (Jarno's words unmistakably bring *Hamlet* to mind!) and the Society of the Tower. It is the tension of the *Nacheinander* of plot, of actual living, and the *Nebeneinander* of coexisting possibilities within human existence. Human wholeness is by definition an abstraction from the individuated, concrete practicalities that actual living involves. If it is expressible, it is so either in discursive formulation (the Society of the Tower) or in symbolic images, as in Natalie's Hall of the Past, where art makes possible "something by which the whole man felt himself laid hold of" (541). Wilhelm is not allowed, as it were, to take up permanent residence in the Society of the Tower or in the Hall of the Past. To do so would imply a retreat into a bloodless existence of concepts and possibilities. Wilhelm must go on living his life, and this means that he will be part of that maddeningly wayward process in which clarity alternates with bafflement, a sense of purpose with the feeling of incomprehensible randomness. In the deepest sense, then, there is no inalienable attainment of perfect self-knowledge and self-possession.

So how does Goethe's novel end? *Wilhelm Meister's*

---

[10] *Hamburger Ausgabe*, VIII, 520.

Apprenticeship, like *Agathon* before it, closes with a happy ending that is undercut by irony as fairy-tale ease and swiftness takes over.[11] In this way Goethe, like Wieland, provides an ending, as is demanded by the conventions of novel fiction, but also suggests that *such* endings are really only the property of fictions. For this reason, the admission to the Society of the Tower does not come at the end of the novel (just as in Thomas Mann's *The Magic Mountain* the chapter "Snow" does not form the conclusion of the novel). There is an intimation of wholeness, but no climactic attainment of it by the eager but baffled protagonist. In Mann's novel, the glimpse of human wholeness is vouchsafed in a dream, in a special realm that is removed from the contingencies of actual living. Similarly, the Society of the Tower is a special world; it is not claimed that human society in general is like the Society of the Tower. Moreover, the human wholeness to which it is dedicated is contained essentially within the context of discursive formulation. As Georg Lukács has so cogently suggested,[12] it follows from this that *Wilhelm Meister's Apprenticeship* is a novel committed to human wholeness but unable to *show* that human wholeness as an achieved reality—precisely because everyday living involves a restriction of the complex human self to a certain set of practical choices. The result is irony and that reserved position which constantly mediates between the real on the one hand and the potential on the other.

I think it is important to stress the full import of Goethe's irony here. On the whole, criticism of *Wilhelm Meister's Apprenticeship* has tended either to assert the

[11] See Eichner, "Zur Deutung von *Wilhelm Meisters Lehrjahren*," 195ff., for a telling discussion of this point.

[12] In Lukács, *Goethe und seine Zeit*, in Lukács, *Werke*, VII (Neuwied and Berlin, 1964), 69-88. On the political implications of the novel see G-L. Fink, "Die Bildung des Bürgers zum "Bürger": Individuum und Gesellschaft in *Wilhelm Meisters Lehrjahren*," *Recherches Germaniques*, 2 (1972), 3ff.

completed *Bildung* of the hero or to assert that the goal of Wilhelm's journey is rarefied to the point of being bloodless.[13] But Goethe surely wanted to leave this question open. Wilhelm really does not know all the answers by the end of the novel. Jarno, for all his reverential intoning of aphoristic insights, cannot convince Wilhelm, nor can he even cheer him up. The pupil remains obstinately bad-tempered. A mere three pages from the end of the novel, Wilhelm laments his inadequacy and wonders whether he will ever be able to assume proper control of his life: "Again and again have my eyes been opened to my conduct; but it was always too late, always in vain! . . . We are wretched, and destined to be wretched: what does it matter whether blame of ours, higher influence or chance, virtue or vice, wisdom or foolishness plunge us into ruin?" (607). These are hardly the words of a master in the art of living.

Of course, Wilhelm's despair is not the last word. The beneficence of a providentially constituted world comes to his aid: Natalie is to be his, and Wilhelm can hardly conceive his good fortune as the Beautiful Amazon becomes his wife. Ultimately, the novel comes to rest on an article of faith: the world gives the individual the room and the time to grow as his selfhood demands. He is allowed to experiment, and experiment implies the possibility of error. But in the last analysis the world will help him to find himself when he is ready to cope adequately with any given experience. In one sense, then, there is a happy ending, but it is perfunctory because the process of living and erring goes on. Clustering around the curiously indeterminate figure of Wilhelm we see a number of alternative destinies. There are figures whose *raison d'être* is to be found in conven-

---

[13] See Blackall's review of conflicting viewpoints in his *Goethe and the Novel*, 297-99. For contemporary reactions see Klaus Gille, *Wilhelm Meister im Urteil der Zeitgenossen* (Assen, 1971), esp. 341.

tional, practical activity (Werner) or whose fulfillment resides in the inner life (the Beautiful Soul). There are the actors, small-minded, generous, irresponsible, blithe. There are the aristocrats of the Society of the Tower, sententious, energetic, forceful, compassionate. And there are two figures who, for many readers, powerfully dominate the novel: Mignon and the Harper. Their center of gravity is not in the practical social world; rather, their poetic intensity is the measure of their longing for a different world, and of their helpless inability to cope with the actualities around them. The poetry of their being and of their utterances issues from a tragic alienation from the real world. Their unhealthy dislocation is their doom: they are written out of the novel.[14] But they remain as the embodiment of one among many experiential possibilities.

All these figures have their intersection in Wilhelm; they are ciphers for potentialities within him. Wilhelm himself is, as it were, overgenerously endowed with possible existences: hence his characteristic receptivity and indecisiveness. He is unable to choose, to be the decisive arbiter of his own life. This overendowment is both blessing and curse: it makes him a kind of master, somehow richer in being than his fellows, yet a master who, we sense, will have great difficulty in ever calling a halt, in putting his apprenticeship behind him once and for all.

[14] See David Turner's judicious discussion of this aspect in his *"Wilhelm Meisters Lehrjahren* and German Classicism," in *Periods in German Literature*, ed. J. M. Ritchie (London, 1969), 103.

== IV ==
Stifter:
Indian Summer
(1857)

Adalbert Stifter (1805-1868) spent his early years in the Bohemian Forest, and it is this landscape which repeatedly informs his novels and stories. In 1818 he began his schooling at the Benedictine monastery of Kremsmünster in Upper Austria. Here his intelligence was both recognized and encouraged, and he went on to study at the University of Vienna. In spite of his passionate attachment to Fanni Greipl he married Amalia Mohaupt in 1837. For some years he earned his living as a private tutor in well-to-do Viennese houses, but in 1850 he was appointed to a position in educational administration in Linz. For some fifteen years he remained a school inspector in Upper Austria. His last years were darkened by the increasing aridity of his marriage: in their inability to have children he saw a bitter judgment on the total sterility of his and Amalia's relationship, a sterility he tried to exorcise by an unremitting and frequently articulated insistence on the sanctity of marriage. In January 1868, suffering terrible pain, he took his own life. Stifter's art has often been seen as an attempt at a kind of stylized compensation for the dreariness of his life, involving not so much escapism as hectoring insistence on the rightness of those conventional values by which he made himself live. His is a remarkable oeuvre. In one sense, it is characteristic of the provincialism of German fiction compared with the major achievements of nineteenth-century European prose; in another, it is haunting in its thematic and stylistic strenuousness. Paradoxically, that strenuousness serves to intimate the terrors Stifter sought to assuage.

Heinrich Drendorf, a young man greatly interested in botany and geology, spends his summers in the Austrian mountains, drawing and collecting details of the natural landscape which attract his interest. One summer, a storm obliges him to seek shelter at the residence of one Herr von Risach. He is immediately struck by the harmony and orderliness of this house—the Rose House—by the rightness of all its component parts, the furniture, the books, paintings, and *objets d'art*, the scientific and scholarly instruments. Everything in the house, even the very materials from which it is made, breathes a reverence for the given things of the world which appeals very powerfully to Heinrich. After three days he leaves, but he returns on frequent occasions. He meets Mathilde, a close friend of Risach's who lives on a nearby estate, and gradually he comes to know and to fall in love with her daughter Natalie. Risach and Mathilde give their blessing, as do Heinrich's parents. Risach confides the story of his past to Heinrich: he was a tutor in the house of Mathilde's parents; he and Mathilde were in love. Her parents asked them to wait before getting married. Risach agreed, out of respect for the sacred order of family life. But Mathilde would not wait, and resented Risach's acquiescence in the parental decision. So they parted. Mathilde married and had two children, Gustav and Natalie. Risach went into public life, but then withdrew to the country, buying the Rose House. Mathilde arrived later, after the death of her husband, and bought a nearby farm. Hence it comes about that Risach and Mathilde see each other frequently and live out the Indian summer of their love. Natalie and Heinrich are engaged. He goes off on a world tour which lasts two years, and then he returns to the Rose House, where the marriage is celebrated.

The plot of *Indian Summer* is not exactly alive with exciting incidents. Moreover, even the events summarized above are in large measure peripheral to the main concern of the text. The events that matter are not specific,

discrete happenings; rather, they are the recurring processes and activities in which the characters engage.
Narrative space and energy is expended on the house
itself, on how one restores a painting, prunes a garden,
measures the depth of a lake. Human behavior is significant precisely insofar as it is embedded in this
gradualness and continuity of things and objects, of the
natural and man-made environment. In other words,
there is very little human interest, in the accepted sense
of the term, in Stifter's novel. The one obvious exception is the section in which Risach recounts his past, his
love for Mathilde and the breakdown of their relationship. Yet these events are securely embedded in the
past; they function, in part at least, as a kind of cau-
tionary tale, as a model of human aberration and dis-
turbance which throws into relief the rightness of the
present harmony that prevails. The foreground of the
novel, existentially and stylistically, is Risach's Rose
House as a temple enshrining certain values and principles. It is manifestly a limited world, insulated from the
social generality outside, from any contact with urban
society and the stresses and strains of historical and social change. It is a haven in which everything, every object, every detail, is held in a loving framework. And
thereby the physical facts of this world are made to vi-
brate with abiding value: the characters of the novel and
the narrator accord these objects the reverent contemplation and restorative attention commonly reserved for
the work of art. The framework of Risach's world is, in a
sense, the frame around a picture: the context proclaims
the significance achieved by even the most humble detail.

Toward the end of the novel, Heinrich goes on a
world tour:

I went first via Switzerland to Italy; to Venice, Flor-
ence, Rome, Naples, Syracuse, Palermo, Malta.

From Malta I took a ship to Spain which I crossed
from south to north with many detours. I was in
Gibraltar, Granada, Seville, Cordoba, Toledo, Ma-
drid and many other lesser towns. From Spain I
went to France, from there to England, Ireland, and
Scotland, and from there via the Netherlands and
Germany back home. I had been absent for one and
a half months less than two years. It was again
spring when I returned. (811)[1]

This passage is remarkable for its deadness: the deadness is almost comically at variance with what is being
reported. Here, after some five hundred pages of narration, Heinrich actually does something that would
commonly be held to be interesting and exciting. Yet
these experiences are reduced to a mere list reported in
one paragraph, to an empty, cataloguing baldness
which is never applied to the facts of the Rose House.
The facts quicken with experiential affirmation only
when, a few lines later, Heinrich comments on the glory
of the sea—"perhaps the most splendid thing which the
earth has to offer" (811). But for this brief exception, the
passage has an unmistakable inertia to it. Heinrich's description of the duration of his world tour—"I had been
absent [ich war abwesend gewesen] for one and a half
months less than two years"—explains the deadness of
the list. He has been *absent* for nearly two years. The
places visited represent an exile from the centrality of
the Rose House; his tour was an interlude of inauthenticity, of "being away from being," of having left the
all-encompassing ontological and moral strength of the
world of the Rose House. Quite understandably, after
what amounts to a package tour *avant la lettre*, Heinrich
returns with relief to Risach's dwelling.

But then Heinrich always returns with relief to the
Rose House. Early in the novel, after that crucial first

[1] References are to Stifter, *Der Nachsommer*, ed. M. Stefl (Augsburg,
1954).

sojourn with Risach, Heinrich comes from Vienna to the Rose House. Speaking to Risach, he explicitly contrasts the Rose House with the common world of urban life: "It is strange, but when I came from your estate into the city with its concerns, your being was as a fairy tale in my memory, and now that I am here with peace all around me, this being is real again and city life but a fairy tale. The great has become small for me and the small great" (213). His point is that what seems to be real (the city) fades into insubstantiality before the validity of Risach's world. There are two schemes of opposition in this passage: reality and fairy tale, and great and small. Heinrich implies that both worlds have reality, that each is convincing when one is part of it, but that there is a gulf between them. They cannot both be felt to be real at the same time: as one wanes, the other waxes. Despite Risach's reply—"both probably belong—indeed everything belongs to the whole if life is to be full and happy" (213)—the reader is left in no doubt that Risach's world exists in embattled and rightful opposition to the broader social experience beyond its confines. The Rose House, like Stifter's fiction which celebrates it, is built upon a revaluation of human modes of being and doing. Heinrich concedes the common value scale (of "great" and "small"), but goes on to revalue it completely: "The great has become small for me and the small great." These words are spoken early in the novel. The young man who speaks them might seem to be torn between two allegiances, but the conflict is not allowed to assert itself with any real urgency. As I hope to show later, Stifter's novel hardly operates with psychological verisimilitude in its portrayal of Heinrich Drendorf. The young Heinrich has no scruples about abandoning the "greatness" of Vienna for the "smallness" of Risach's secluded haven. Heinrich as narrator is not really a character in any psychologically individuated sense: he is simply the voice of Stifter's article of faith. *Indian*

Summer is artistically of a piece with its moral aim in that it is resistant to common norms of artistic and fictional interest. This constant intimation (as in the lifeless catalogue of the world tour) that *Indian Summer* was written against the general expectations of novel writing makes Stifter's prose the painstaking, yet incandescent, litany that it is.

Risach's morality, the heart of that litany, is one that esteems the gradual unfolding of the natural world and that attempts to house man within this sacramental gradualness. In human terms, this means the embedding of man in the continuity of the sacred, eternal sequence of family life. If man can be absorbed into that gradualness, then he may become part of the self-renewing whole that is creation itself. But this is not easy. Man is problematic, individuated, and therefore prone to aberration. Hence the stylistic intensity lavished on things: things are simply more trustworthy than people. Risach has an infinite reverence for natural objects, and for the way in which man can serve them through the work of his hands. This involves an ethos of craftmanship, an *artistic* reverence which spills out beyond the *objet d'art* alone to become the *raison d'être* of the Rose House.

Art, as expressed in the total work that is Risach's house, is in every sense premeditated and carefully wrought. It is not a spontaneous expression of individual selfhood. Rather, it springs from an act of human submission before the *donnée* of any given material or experience. Art, therefore, is not hostile to the common universe of humble things and uses: in Hegel's terms, prose and poetry interlock. A wooden floor can be as much a work of art as a statue. Moreover, for Risach, art is part of an overall moral design: it is an expression of right living, of man's offering reverence to the given world of his surroundings and to the fundamental law of gradual continuity which makes that world possible.

Art, then, grows out of a deep-seated human need: "the artist makes his work as the flower blooms: it blooms even if it is in the desert and no eye ever falls upon it" (617). Art is part of the organic self-realization of man; it is the cipher of man's humanity. "In art," Risach comments, "if such modest things merit the name of art, a dislocation [Sprung] is as impossible as in nature" (289). The lack of "Sprünge," of jumps, cracks, fissures, breaks, is the measure of the ontological strength of the art in question. For art, like every other aspect of man's life, must obey that general law "that in creation gradualness is always pure and wise" (289).

Man's significance depends, ultimately, on his oneness with that gradualness. The story told by *Indian Summer* is that of Heinrich's gradual absorption into this order of being. The events are recounted in the first person by a young man who comes to the Rose House from the world outside, and who is inevitably drawn to identify that house as *the* world. The Heinrich Drendorf who first comes to the Rose House has reverence for things; he is, we learn, particularly interested in the natural sciences. He also has profound respect for the family. Risach helps him to round out these two spheres, the human and the scientific, to the point where they merge into the overarching unity of a total moral vision. Heinrich learns from Risach, but the learning process is serene, gradual, inevitable. There is no friction, no resentment, no willfulness in Heinrich. Even when Heinrich as narrator asserts the distance that separated him from Risach, we never quite believe him. The present, narrating self dominates completely, and its acknowledgment and stylistic enactment of Risach's principles is unambiguous. A characteristic moment between mentor and pupil has Risach speaking:

"Because men only want and cherish one thing, because they pursue the one-sided in order to find satisfaction, they make themselves unhappy. If we were in order within ourselves, then we would take much greater pleasure in the things of this earth. But when an excess of wishes and cravings takes possession of us, we always hear them speaking and are unable to perceive the innocence of the things around us. Unfortunately, we describe things as important when they are the objects of our passions, and as unimportant when they stand in no relation to these passions, whereas the opposite can often be the truth."

I did not then understand these words so well. I was still too young and I myself often heard only my inner self speaking—and not the things around me. (213)

Heinrich's immaturity is anything but problematic. It is occasionally referred to, but it is never evoked with any stylistic urgency. He is the perfect pupil, and Risach the perfect teacher. Lessons are profferred and absorbed evenly and inevitably. Other people (Natalie) will be there as and when they are needed. There is, quite simply, no friction, no tension, no individuated psychological interest. The human sphere, although it is the center of the novel's purpose, remains curiously unspoken. The urgency of thoroughgoing narrative attention is directed toward things, toward the celebration of a number of modest practical activities. This is the extraordinary radicalism of Stifter's achievement: things are handled with a greater stylistic intensity than are people. People can stray from the norm, but things *are* the norm.

There is, of course, one exception to this rule, the story of Risach's love for Mathilde. It is the story of human aberration, of a love thrown away because of impetuosity on Mathilde's part, because of excessive diffidence and self-control on Risach's part. This past gives a dark relief to the harmony of the Rose House. But the darkness is exorcised by being contained in

Heinrich's narration of how it is possible for youth to accept the wisdom and maturity of old age without having to go through the process of error itself. Even for Risach and Mathilde the sting of tragedy is taken out of their past experiences. They have come together late in life; the summer may have been thrown away, but there is an Indian summer. In Risach's account of the crowning of their love, there is an explicit revaluation of the modes of human affection. The Indian summer is *not* second best. Rather, it is an all-too-rare perfection:

> There is a marital love which follows upon the days of that fiery, stormy love which takes man to woman: it appears as quiet, totally sincere, sweet friendship, which is beyond all praise and all blame, and which is perhaps the nearest thing to mirrorlike clarity which human relations can achieve. This love came. It is heartfelt, without self-seeking, it takes pleasure in the company of the other, it seeks to adorn and to lengthen his days, it is tender and has, as it were, no earthly source to it. Mathilde shares all my concerns. She walks with me through the rooms of my house, she is with me in the garden, looks at the flowers and vegetables, she is in the farm and watches its milk yield, she goes into the carpenter's shop and observes what we are doing, and she shares in our art and even in our scientific pursuits. I keep an eye on her house, I look at the things in the residence, in the farm, in the fields, I share her wishes and views, and I took the education and future of her children to my heart. So we live in joy and constancy our, as it were, Indian summer, without having known the preceding summer. (779-80)

The key verbs here are "to share," "to be," "to look at." The love is praised in moral terms which recall the vision of Christian charity in 1 Cor. 13. Yet embedded within the passage are many practical details which suggest what activities this love entails, how it operates. There are facts, aspects of human behavior that are at one with this love. They amount to sharing interests, to walking round the house, the garden, the outbuildings, to looking at the things that are there.

For Risach and Mathilde, this wisdom was distilled out of error. For Heinrich, it represents a by-passing of youth, a shortcut to the Indian summer. Stifter seeks to persuade us of something that at first sight appears inherently self-contradictory: the Rose House in all its manifest restriction of human experience nevertheless allows for the realization of the whole man, of the totality of human aspiration. Indeed—and here is the essential paradox—the wholeness is only made possible by a drastic restriction of the self and its concerns.

Both thematically and stylistically, *Indian Summer* is manifestly a challenge to all manner of common assumptions and expectations. As W. H. Bruford so cogently points out,[2] it is a novel written against history, yet written in an age that was obsessed with historicism. It betrays no interest in national or social problems, it allows for no questioning of the ethics of early retirement to a quasi-feudal existence in the countryside.[3] There is no awareness of the stresses and strains of modern life, of incipient industrialization, of the increasing specialization and narrowing of man's capacities in the practicality of his social life. It is a novel that devalues all manner of human qualities that are commonly held to be significant—vitality, passion, conflict. It is a novel written against the demands of plot in that it attempts to transform man from an individuated entity into a being who exists in utopian oneness with the ontological in-

[2] Bruford, *The German Tradition of Self-Cultivation* (Cambridge, 1975), 142.

[3] See Roy Pascal's telling discussion of this point, in *The German Novel* (Manchester, 1956), 64.

tegrity of things. Its unmistakably stylized narrative betrays no interest in the psychological resonance of first-person narration.[4] There is no real tension between experiencing self and narrating self; there is only the systematic exorcism of common narrative and psychological expectation.

Within the context of nineteenth-century fiction, *Indian Summer* is a truly remarkable work. It is an attempt at epic totality, at oneness of facts and values, of existence and significance, that can only be achieved by the restriction of its whole concern to one overtly sacramental enclave. Within the narrow world of the Rose House we find a realm in which nature, art, and ethics are at one.[5] Only a few years later, Gustave Flaubert was to write *Bouvard and Pécuchet*, the counterimage to *Indian Summer*. In Flaubert's novel, the protected world of humble activities and simple things congeals into grotesque bourgeois clutter. But Stifter uncompromisingly produced a novel in which limitation is transfigured into totality, in which everything man needs to know and be is realized in the modest doings of the Rose House. It is probably tempting to see *Indian Summer* as a somewhat peripheral and provincial phenomenon within the European context. But I would argue that this does not do justice to the resonance of Stifter's novel. The line in lyric poetry, from the intense outpourings of Romanticism via the attempt at motionless, static art of *l'art pour l'art*, to Rilke's concern to remove the human dynamic from poetry in order to rediscover the wholeness of things, is one of the cardinal experiences of the Euro-

---

[4] See V. Lange's discussion of this aspect, in *"Der Nachsommer,"* in *Der deutsche Roman*, ed. B. von Wiese, II (Düsseldorf, 1963), 43ff.

[5] The most suggestive of recent studies concerned with this aspect are in my view: Gerald Gillespie, "Ritualism and Motivic Development in Adalbert Stifter's *Der Nachsommer*," *Neophilologus*, 48 (1964), 312ff.; C. Sjögren, *The Marble Statue as Idea: Collected Essays on Adalbert Stifter's "Der Nachsommer"* (Chapel Hill, 1972); and M-U. Lindau, *Stifters "Der Nachsommer": Ein Roman der verhaltenen Rührung* (Bern, 1973).

pean nineteenth century. Stifter's novel is, it seems to me, part of this imaginative undertaking. As a *novel*, it probably fails. But then, because it was deliberately written against novel expectations, it concedes its failure while at the same time it questions the criteria for success or failure in the accepted novel mode. In a strange way, it is not harmed by its failure, for, as Risach observes, "the artist makes his work as the flower blooms: it blooms even if it is in the desert and no eye ever falls upon it" (617). If the world is not *there* for man, it is not harmed by man's ignorance of it (just as Rilke's things are not diminished by man's ignorance of them).

Indian Summer is different from any of the other Bildungsromane with which I am concerned in that it resolves rather than enacts that tension between restriction and totality, between the *Nacheinander* of plot and the *Nebeneinander* of the human self in all its value-heavy complexity. For Stifter there cannot be even an approximation toward human wholeness within the framework of everyday society. Accordingly, he created an alternative world, one not less, but more confined than the society he so utterly repudiated. Within that world, the limitation of human and artistic interest to a number of simple, practical activities is underwritten by an urgent, almost hectoring, sense of human and artistic wholeness. In the process, prosaic reality comes alive with the poetry of the morally and aesthetically valuable. But the overall tone is one of sacramental pedantry: the difficulty of Stifter's narrative undertaking implies a tension which the act of aesthetic exorcism cannot allay. The attempt to write an unproblematic Bildungsroman in fact serves to intimate the increasing tension to which the genre is prone, a tension which can only be resolved by converting the novel into a monolithic litany.

═ V ═
Keller:
Green Henry
(1879-1880)

Gottfried Keller (1819-1890) lost his father at an early age. His mother maintained the family by letting rooms. Keller attended the local school, but was expelled in 1834, and the injustice of this long haunted him. He determined to become a painter, and after spending some time with relations, he returned to Zurich, where he began his training. In 1840 he went to Munich, but his dreams of making his way as a painter were frustrated by a combination of poverty and lack of talent. He returned home in 1842. In 1848 a grant from the canton enabled him to spend about two years in Heidelberg, where the influence of Ludwig Feuerbach's teaching served to undermine his religious faith. From Hermann Hettner's lectures at the university he learned to appreciate Goethe and the value of literature, particularly drama. Between 1850 and 1855 he lived in Berlin, where he began writing in earnest. When he returned to Zurich in 1855, he found that he had established a certain literary reputation. In 1861 he was appointed Chief Clerk of his home canton. For the next fifteen years he conscientiously discharged all the duties that went with the post, living quietly with his mother and then with his sister during this time. He resigned his post in 1876 in order to devote himself entirely to his writing.

The decisive events of Keller's life have been incorporated into his major novel, *Green Henry*. What is important for our purposes, however, is the way the novel explores the underlying tension of Keller's persona. As a prose writer, Keller is one of the great masters of

nineteenth-century German literature. He can be genuinely funny, and his humor embraces a whole spectrum from the serene and conciliatory to the mordant
and grotesque. Above all, Keller's prose has a sheer
vitality that seems curiously at variance with his somewhat joyless life, particularly with that very long coda
during which he followed the routine of the irreproachable bureaucrat. Out of the conflict between imaginative potential on the one hand, and the constrictions of
practical social living on the other, *Green Henry*, as I
hope to show, derives its principal import.

Heinrich Lee loses his father at the age of five and is
brought up by his mother. In school he suffers from the
poverty of his home background, and he seeks to offset
his disadvantages by stealing money from a chest of
silver coins which his father left him. He is a child of
imaginative disposition, and he is often able to turn this
to good account, finding that he can on occasion replace
fact by fiction and get away with it (as in the incident
when he gets older boys into trouble by accusing them
of having taught him swear words). His desire for prominence in the school leads him—against his better
judgment—to take part in a procession attacking an unpopular schoolteacher; as a result, he is expelled. Heinrich attempts to pursue a career as a painter, but his
studies are interrupted when his mother sends him on a
visit to her home village. There Heinrich meets and is
attracted to two very different women: the spiritual,
ethereal Anna, and the robust, sensuous Judith. On re-
turning home, Heinrich does genuinely improve his
painting by becoming the pupil of the unstable but
gifted artist Römer. But a break soon comes in their relationship when Heinrich discovers that his teacher has
been involved in financially dubious activities. In a fit of
self-righteousness, Heinrich demands the return of a
loan, thereby bankrupting Römer, who later is commit-

ted to a madhouse. Heinrich continues to visit his mother's relatives. Anna, his idealized beloved, dies, but her image continues to exert a potent influence on him, with the result that he repudiates Judith. She leaves Switzerland and emigrates to America.

Heinrich goes to Munich to pursue his artistic career. But his attempts are dogged by failure. On learning that his mother is gravely ill, he leaves for home. He is given hospitality on the way by a Count who knows and has been collecting Heinrich's sketches (which Heinrich has been forced to sell for a song to a junk store dealer). The Count has a foster child, Dortchen Schönfund, who clearly falls in love with Heinrich and he with her. But Heinrich is unable to pluck up the courage to propose to her. He resumes his journey home, arriving in time to witness the death of his mother. Heinrich now abandons all pretensions to an artistic career. He becomes a civil servant and spends the rest of his life in the service of his community. His loneliness is alleviated somewhat by the return of Judith from America: they agree not to marry, but to remain firm and frank friends.

Such is the essential outline of the largely autobiographical plot of Keller's novel. One should note at the outset that there are two versions of the novel. The first (1854-1855), written in the third person with a lengthy first-person interpolation, is in many ways more passionate and intense than the later version (1879-1880), which is narrated in the first person. The earlier version ends with the death of the hero from grief and shame: Heinrich is obliged to recognize that both practical social reality and his artistic aspirations are insufficient to sustain his existence. The second version has (as the summary above indicates) a more conciliatory conclusion, and indeed, the conciliating mode of the recollecting hero-narrator does remove some of the friction and urgency from the incidents recounted. For this reason, many readers have felt that the first version is to be preferred. They argue that the first version, precisely because it is sustained in third person narrative, allows Keller to explore his own experience with a distance, with an imaginative radicalism, that he never allowed himself in life. There is undeniably a certain lifelessness to the closing sections of the second version, which chronicle the protagonist's espousal of the irreproachable ethic of bureaucratic hard work. Hence, one cannot dismiss out of hand the view that the later version is debilitated by being narratively too close to Keller's own evasiveness and timorousness.

Yet one must, in my view, recognize that Keller in the later version makes no attempt to claim more for the experiences depicted in its closing chapters than is appropriate. The Dortchen Schönfund episode makes abundantly clear that, in spite of his many potentialities, Heinrich is simply unable to convert his inner feelings into practical, outward expression (that is, a relationship). Deadness is the price Heinrich pays for that continuous divorcing of his imaginative life from social reality. And, as Roy Pascal and Wolfgang Preisendanz have shown in their magnificent studies of Keller's novel,[1] this deadness is part of the central thematic concern of *Green Henry*. The novel chronicles the life of a young man whose imagination in childhood becomes so much the colorful supplanter of a drab reality that he spends the rest of his life unable to find an assent to reality that goes beyond the grudging and the pragmatic. As Pascal so well suggests,[2] it is in this thematic sense that Heinrich's progression along this road has profound sociopsychological implications: in all his eccentricity, Heinrich becomes representative of larger social issues and problems in a way that the first version, for all its greater

---

[1] Pascal, *The German Novel* (Manchester, 1956), 30ff.; Preisendanz, "*Der grüne Heinrich*," in *Der deutsche Roman*, ed. B. von Wiese, II (Düsseldorf, 1963), 82ff.

[2] Pascal, *German Novel*, 35.

immediacy, cannot allow him to be. Moreover, it is the measure of the thematic resonance of the second version that we are confronted not with a simple dualism of imagination *versus* reality, but with their dialectical interaction and interpenetration. Imagination can be an escapist compensation, but it can also be the vital agent by which the contingent facts of a social environment are rounded out into the density of an embracing human reality.

Green Henry opens with one of the several crucial passages in which Keller evokes the continuity of life within the human community. Remarkably, we are told first of the graveyard, of the soil to which each inhabitant returns. This humus, we learn, is not alien to man; it is made up of the bones of his ancestors, so that even in death he inhabits the continuity of village existence:

> The little graveyard, which surrounds the church, its whitewash still glowing despite its age, has never been extended: its earth consists literally of the dissolved bones of previous generations: it is impossible that even to a depth of ten feet there should be a grain of that earth that has not undertaken its journey through the human organism, that has not been turned over with the rest of the earth. (III, 1-2)[3]

It is from this kind of existential shelter that Heinrich Lee will increasingly remove himself, thereby producing an isolation that will amount to devastating homelessness. The narrator can celebrate and esteem this human possibility. But as we shall see, the protagonist is unable to find such an affirmative relationship to the modest facts of social continuity. Out of this narrative

[3] References throughout are to Keller, *Sämtliche Werke*, ed. J. Fränkel, III-VI (Zurich and Munich, 1926). Roman numerals indicate the volume number, followed by the page number in arabic.

tension—between the "then," experiencing self and the "now," narrating self—the novel generates its principal import.

We come next to the account of Heinrich's school days. We note the gaiety and fantasy of the child, and the authoritarian incomprehension of the elders, with their rudimentary—and largely outward—notions of right and wrong. On the first day in school Heinrich is asked with his fellows to name the letters of the alphabet. He has heard the word *Pumpernickel* at home and is fascinated by its sound. As ill-luck has it, he is asked to name the letter P, which he promptly identifies as "Pumpernickel." The unconventional reply lands him with a severe beating. The teacher shows no comprehension of the complex psychological processes of a child's mind: capital letters are shapes, words are sounds, mysterious entities in their own right, whose conventional value has not yet been learned or absorbed. By definition, the growing-up process involves an accommodation to the established universe of terms, of linguistic, social, and moral conventions. Yet the adult world seems unaware that in the act of accommodation individual fantasy and established rules can be reconciled. Instead, adults proceed by brute force, riding roughshod over the child's unformed self-understanding—and thereby, as the interpolated "Meretlein" incident makes clear, they can produce the self-destructive defiance of aberrant behavior. Heinrich's experience of religious instruction is particularly telling in this context. He is intelligent enough to perceive that God is defined by his elders and betters as a kind of ultimate arbiter of socially acceptable behavior. Against this God Heinrich rebels in agonized blasphemy. His blasphemy is a nervous act, born of a fear that the divinity does exist and will punish if provoked. And in a sense, the punishment would be a comfort: he would know what he was up against, he would have proved the issue one way or the other. Once again, the psychic processes within the child display a complex dialectic of acknowledgment and rejection, of association and dissociation vis-à-vis the values of the adult world.

It is, of course, the measure of Heinrich's imaginative skill and intelligence that he is able, in the swearing incident, to concoct a fantasy instantly acceptable to the adult world. Moreover, he senses that the teachers are so narrow-minded in their understanding of swearing that they will not for a moment reflect on the complexity of the phenomenon. They will punish the behavior without inquiring into its causes. Heinrich knows he is producing a fiction that is both more simple and more colorful than the reality of the situation. Thereby he can manipulate both the "real" world of adult simplification and the complex reality of his own psychic processes. As a result, his imaginative act appears powerful and dangerous. The swearing incident suggests the sheer power of the child's affective and imaginative life. This is underpinned by the whole sequence of events involving Meierlein. Heinrich's desire to have money, to be part of the schoolboy group, leads him to borrow money from Meierlein, the young moneylender. Heinrich is appalled by the bureaucratic and monetary implacability of his adversary, and the hatred he stores up for Meierlein never loses its edge. Not even the passage of time dulls it: Heinrich will rejoice when he hears of Meierlein's death many years later. Here, as elsewhere in the novel, we sense a perception—rarely expressed with such force in the Bildungsroman tradition—of the finality of experience. Heinrich's relentless hatred has indelible contours: the emotional intensity of childhood, as Keller portrays it, includes something disturbing and unsettling. It is never allowed to soften into a sentimental idyll. Moreover, Keller leaves us in no doubt that Heinrich is endangered throughout his adolescent years. He is someone who is both apart from his fellows and yet longs to be one of their number. The incident with the unpopular teacher which leads to his expulsion from school shows the uneasy spectrum of Heinrich's motivation: from being the skeptical outsider he gradually maneuvers himself (and is maneuvered) into the role of quasi ringleader. Here we sense the imbalance of his relationship to reality: he is withdrawn and critical; yet when he is involved, it is with an excessive commitment by which he seeks to maximize his acceptance. Keller offers a remarkably subtle and differentiated understanding of the issues involved. The moral question—whether Heinrich or his rather narrow environment is to blame—is not, as Beddow would have us believe,[4] the primary concern. Keller's unforgettable portrayal of childhood suggests precisely the problematic area of interaction between individual imagination and social norms that makes Heinrich's fate the exceptional enactment of issues inherent in the social generality around him. His psychological dislocations are symptomatic of the social uncertainties embedded in bourgeois idealism.

When Heinrich goes to visit his mother's relatives, his life acquires two centers in the contrasting figures of Anna and Judith. Anna is beautiful and frail. Heinrich's attraction to her, it has often been maintained, is an idealistic one: there is, for example, a persistent awkwardness about the physical aspects of their relationship. This culminates in the kiss after the carnival, which so troubles Anna that she faints, and which afterwards leaves them both with feelings of guilt and shame. For Heinrich, Anna more and more becomes a kind of disembodied wraith, someone to whom he can pour out all his wish-dreams, all his visions of human nobility and purity—in short, all his imaginative fan-

---

[4] Michael Beddow, "Thomas Mann's *Felix Krull* and the Traditions of the Picaresque Novel and the Bildungsroman" (Ph.D. diss., Cambridge University, 1975), 149ff.

tasies. The unreality of the relationship is precisely the
source of its hold over Heinrich. It is a relationship that
cannot grow with time, with the development of physical maturity: Anna always remains the childhood
sweetheart of the first awkwardly solemn kiss by the
grave of the grandmother. In this early scene the narrator beautifully suggests the theme of human continuity with which the novel opens: the gaiety of the
young people, the joy in physical movement, in danc-
ing, coexists with the death and burial of the grand-
parent. But from this point on, the relationship between
Heinrich and Anna becomes increasingly ethereal. And
it is essentially because of this appeal of the physically
inadequate and insubstantial that Heinrich repudiates
Judith.

For Judith he feels an immediate, natural attraction
which he simply will not allow himself to trust. Yet—
and this is the greatness of Keller's achievement—Judith
is not just a cipher for physical vitality, womanhood,
and spontaneous sensuality. On her first appearance in
the novel, Judith is associated with natural growth, with
apples, milk, the yield of the harvest. But she also has a
mind, an intelligence of unshakable perception and
tenacity, a moral sense imbued with the honesty of her
physical existence. In the superlative scene at the end of
Book II, Chapter 18, Heinrich is impelled to declare his
love for Judith, but he does so in restrictive terms:

> For Anna I would bear every burden and obey her
> every sign; for her sake I would like to become a
> good and honorable man, transparent like a crystal.
> I would do nothing without thinking of her, and to
> all eternity I would be at one with her soul even if I
> were never to see her again from this day forward!
> All this I could not do for you. And yet I love you
> with all my heart, and if you were to ask me to
> prove it by letting you plunge a knife into my heart,

> I would stand quite still before you now and calmly
> allow my blood to flow over your lap! (IV, 230-31)

This declaration of love, behind the grand rhetoric of the adolescent, amounts to an exaltation of Anna and a debasement of Judith. The feelings for Anna have to do with sublimity, integrity, eternal devotion; those for Judith are linked with passion and desperation. Judith's reply, amidst tears, is characteristic in its honesty: "What am I supposed to do with your blood! Ah, never has a man wished to be good, clean, and pure before me, and yet I love truth as I do myself!" (IV, 231). The truth Judith esteems is a moral value that is immanent in her very being, in actual living; it is not a luxuriant fantasy divorced from the real. Yet men, specifically Heinrich, will not allow themselves to see this, are ashamed of their attraction to her. The result is a dualist heresy, one which divorces the real from the valuable. The dangers inherent in Heinrich's childhood are beginning to bear fruit. And that childhood, we remember, was shaped not simply by the facts of Heinrich's personal psychology, but also by his all-important contacts with the adult social world, in particular by his school experiences. The imperfectly understood relationship between the demands of practical social living on the one hand, and the claims of the imaginative capacity in the individual on the other, emerges as an inadequacy not only in Heinrich but also in his teachers. We note, furthermore, that the dualism which vitiates Heinrich's sexual relationship with Judith is not confined to him alone. He is, apparently, one of a number of suitors whose idealism forces a debasement of the physical attraction felt for Judith. The result is a double impoverishment: ideals become vague and unfocused, actuality is dismissed as a suffocating dimension. In this sense, the troubled course of Heinrich's feelings for Judith is more than simply a personal experience.

Rather, it focuses a complex of themes that has general social relevance. That complex is the inquiry into the relationship of practical living on the one hand and the individual's creative inwardness on the other. It is the center of the Bildungsroman genre, and it has its roots in the vital intellectual issues of bourgeois society.[5]

The particular significance of Heinrich's curiously resentful dependence on Judith expresses itself in their conversations, which serve to articulate the whole spectrum of Heinrich's troubled relationship to social reality. One occasion is especially important. Heinrich goes to Judith after his betrayal of Römer. He seeks absolution from her, he hopes to shed his bad conscience. What Judith offers him is a combination of astringency and compassion that he cannot deal with:

> The reproaches of your conscience are a healthy diet for you, and on this bread you can chew for the rest of your days without my spreading the butter of forgiveness on it! And I could not even do it; because what cannot be changed is not for that reason to be forgotten, to my way of thinking, and I have experienced it often enough! By the way, I do not unfortunately feel that you have become repulsive to me because of what you have done. What are we here for if not to love people for what they are? (v, 67)

Judith clearly expresses the sense that Heinrich has incurred guilt through his experience. She returns to it a few lines later: "you are now grown up, and in this

[5] For a different illumination of precisely these issues see Flaubert's *Sentimental Education* (1869). Keller is, I think, more generous both to his protagonist and to the world of mid-nineteenth-century bourgeois society than is Flaubert. Whereas Keller can consistently imply the possibility—and the validity—of mediation between social facts and inward selfhood, Flaubert operates with an acrid polarization of the vague, self-aggrandizing fantasies of Frédéric on the one hand, and the vapidity and meretriciousness of contemporary society on the other. Both reality and the imagination are, it seems, utterly tainted.

transaction you have already lost your moral virginity" (v, 68). She asserts here the growth process that is part of the traditional Bildungsroman pattern. In this sense, she could be seen as a kind of mentor figure. Yet the emphasis of her teaching is remarkable within the context of the Bildungsroman because it asserts the irrevocable nature of experience. She insists, in effect, that other people do not exist simply for the educative benefit of Heinrich; they exist in their own right. Moreover, the interaction between Heinrich and them is binding: human actions have effects, they produce results which are lasting. Judith confronts Heinrich with the fact that his life is not just an experiment which allows him to find himself in his own good time. The destruction of Römer is a fact for which Heinrich will continue to bear moral responsibility. Römer will not, as it were, recur once Heinrich has learned his lesson: he is not a figure embedded in a beneficently providential world organized for the protagonist's benefit. And yet Judith, having issued this moral judgment, does not withdraw her affection for Heinrich. Rather, she asserts her love for him as a moral involvement which is not conditional upon good behavior. Her physicality produces more than a sensual response to the moment, an unreflected instinctuality. Rather, it is a moral truthfulness derived from physical love. But this is something Heinrich cannot acknowledge because it does not belong in his imaginative scenario. Judith's words of love—"what are we here for if not to love people for what they are"—touch the sore point. Heinrich is unable to love the world as it is, to love Judith as she is, to be loved as he is. He has lived too long in a frame of mind in which the real is insufficient when measured against inward criteria. His imagination will tell him that he must repudiate Judith in the name of an ideal. The key image associated with Anna is the star: her very unattainability makes her precious. In her he sees "such a clear and lovely star for my whole life . . . according to

which all my actions can be shaped" (v, 89). We recall
the moment when Heinrich, having kissed Judith, reflects on the difference between her kisses and Anna's:
"This difference was so palpable that in the midst of violent kisses Anna's star rose" (iv, 232).

From the time of Wieland's *Agathon* and Goethe's
Wilhelm Meister, the German Bildungsroman has been
concerned with somewhat naively idealistic young men
who grope their way toward some recognition of the
real in its significance. But no novel in the tradition has
so powerfully documented the moral danger of unfocused idealism as does *Green Henry*. It is, moreover, part
of the intensity of Keller's novel that the narrator perceives what it was not given to the experiencing self to
understand and to act upon. In the context of Judith's
remarks about the irreversibility of time and experience,
this narrative technique acquires an ominous ring.
When Heinrich turns away from Judith, we wonder
whether that betrayal will ever prove redeemable.

If the relationships with Anna and Judith highlight
the intrapersonal consequences of Heinrich's inability to
love and trust the real, the two scenes depicting popular
festivals (one in Switzerland, one in Munich) illustrate
the broader social consequences of Heinrich's in-
capacities. The Swiss celebrations, which culminate in a
performance of *Wilhelm Tell*, are portrayed by the narrator with great honesty and unsentimentality. Indeed,
it is this very down-to-earthness of the Swiss carnival
that offends the youthful Heinrich. He is appalled that
everyday reality—haggling over money—should so
overtly mingle with the high flights of patriotic and poetic drama. Yet his fastidiousness is profoundly wrong:
the *Tell* performance is the expression of that imaginative allegiance to their community which makes the vil-
lagers so much more than separate individuals out for
their own benefit. The coexistence of the overtly practical and the imaginative is unacceptable to Heinrich be-

cause of the disjunction of precisely those two realms within himself. This dislocation also determines the limitation of Heinrich's art: his painting and sketching is either so fussy and painstaking that the object or scene copied becomes a labyrinth of minute strokes,[6] or it becomes vague and sentimental as the imagination renounces any concrete embodying of its vision. Precisely that middle ground, Heinrich discovers, is occupied by Goethe's art, although this insight does not serve to transform Heinrich's artistic capacities. What moves Heinrich about Goethe is the latter's ability to render the immanent poetry of the real, "something poetic or, which means the same thing, something living and sensible" (v, 7). Heinrich is overwhelmed by Goethe's "outgoing love for everything that has come about and lasts, a love which honors the rightness and the significance of every thing and which feels the connection and the depth of the world" (v, 5). The interpenetration of the concrete and the imaginative is, of course, precisely the strength and beauty of the Swiss *Wilhelm Tell* performance. That strength is highlighted by the description of the Munich carnival Heinrich attends. It is meretricious in its consciously arty quality: the pseudo-medievalism is the archly imaginative veneer covering a squalid and largely trivial actuality. All this is typified in the duel, the absurdly grandiloquent and inflated imaginative gesture overlaying small-mindedness and irritability.

Increasingly, Munich seems unable to provide the sustenance Heinrich is seeking. There are glimpses of possible fulfillment: the friendships with specific individuals, the anatomy classes which reveal to Heinrich the miracle of organic reality. But no epiphany is forth-

[6] For a discussion of "labyrinth" imagery in the novel see F. J. Stopp, "Keller's *Der grüne Heinrich*: The Pattern of the Labyrinth," in *The Discontinuous Tradition: Studies in Honour of E. L. Stahl*, ed. P. F. Ganz (Oxford, 1971), 129ff.

coming; the world constantly refuses to oblige Heinrich
with the desired experiences and satisfactions. News of
his mother's ill health obliges him to return to Switzerland. On several occasions he has dreamed of his homeland, even glimpsing its possible beauty and significance as a constantly changing continuity, as a sacred
and sustaining sequence of generations. But even the
return home does not provide the fulfillment, the sense
of rightness and integrity that Heinrich looks for. The
clock cannot be put back; Heinrich has to pay for the falsity of his imaginative life, for the relentless encapsula-
tion from reality that has resulted from it. One feels this
also in the episode with Dortchen Schönfund. Indeed, it
is almost as though novel convention becomes an overt
presence here: we have the aristocratic environment,
the good will toward the hero, the loving girl. We wonder whether the conclusion of Goethe's *Wilhelm Meister's Apprenticeship* is not being resurrected here. But the
experiences we observe do not allow of any such resur-
rection: Heinrich is the "frozen Christ" (vii, 210). The
inward life, the imaginative possibility, is there, but no
outward enaction takes place. Heinrich cannot break
this deadness which surrounds him, and he loses
Dortchen irrevocably. Heinrich is, we remember, the
man who carries around with him the skull of Albertus
Zwiehahn, the emblem of a withered and wasted life.

Heinrich returns to Switzerland. Whatever his dream
images of his homeland, the reality he experiences lags
far behind. But then, for Heinrich, reality has always
lagged far behind. The death of his mother produces
guilt in him, and this in turn leads to emptiness, to the
sense of watching himself dying: "it was almost as
though my own self moved out of me" (vi, 296). There
is the last flickering of an attempt to make contact with
living relationships: "while the lament for my mother
gradually became a dark, but quietly even, background
of joylessness, the image of Dorothea [Dortchen] began

to assert itself with greater liveliness—but without bringing light into the darkness" (VI, 301). He finally plucks up courage to write to Dortchen's father. His letter is oblique, diffident—and late. The reply confirms that he is *too* late: Dortchen is engaged. So Heinrich becomes "a somewhat monosyllabic and melancholy civil servant" (VI, 308). This is the dominant note at the close of the novel.

That note is intensified by the final episode, the return of Judith from America. Her reappearance does alleviate somewhat Heinrich's isolation and anguish. Once again he confides in her, hoping for absolution. Once again Judith insists that she can only offer him her affection:

> "Tell me everything, but do not think that I shall be turned against you."
> "But then your judgment has no value if it is conditioned by your kindness and affection."
> "But this affection is enough of a judgment and you must accept it. Now tell me." (VI, 319-20)

Judith's moral toughness is the same as before. Heinrich would like to transform her into an arbiter who measures with some yardstick other than human affection and involvement. But this Judith cannot become. She insists on the integrity and truth of her feelings for Heinrich: she will not allow herself to be transformed into some *dea ex machina*, into some spiritual authority divorced from the real world.

In her affection for Heinrich, Judith retains the clearsightedness that has characterized so much of her behavior. She insists that it would be wrong for them to marry: "We will forego [entsagen] that crown and instead we will be the more certain of that happiness which delights us at this moment" (VI, 323). The term *entsagen* sounds very hallowed and Goethean. Yet it has a specific moral rightness here, for it implies that the clock cannot be turned back. In Keller's novel there is no Indian summer without the preceding summer. Neither Heinrich nor Judith can undo what has become of their relationship. Just as Judith had insisted that she could not judge with eyes other than those of a woman who knows and feels what it is given to her to know and to feel, so now she perceives that neither of them can get outside the context and function of their own selfhood. Keller's novel has the honesty to recognize that the past life is not an experiment preparing the individual for right knowledge, for full maturity. It is binding, not only morally, but also psychologically, in the sense that what a man has been and done inalienably molds and defines his selfhood at any given time.

Judith dies some years later. Heinrich inherits from her the account he has written of his early years: "According to her wishes, I have now received it from her papers, and have added the other part in order to walk once again the old green paths of memory" (vi, 325). The novel closes with a definition of Heinrich as narrator: in the act of recounting his life he is to celebrate the green paths of memory, the greenness suggesting life, vitality, fertility. The narrator is able to see and cherish what the experiencing self was not able to affirm and realize (in both senses of the word). It is the narrator who perceives the strength of the human community, the resonance of the *Wilhelm Tell* pageant, the glory of Judith. To so much of this the experiencing Heinrich was impervious. The interplay between the experiencing self and the narrating self gives a toughness and astringency to the whole work. The artistic (narrative) achievement is not allowed to take the sting out of the actual experiences chronicled. We are aware both of Heinrich's slow strangling of his own living substance, and of the vibrant reality around him. To modify an observation of Kafka's, one might say that there is hope everywhere—but not for Heinrich Lee.

I have on several occasions referred to ways in which Keller's novel departs from the Bildungsroman tradition as we have observed it in works of Wieland, Goethe, and Stifter. Above all, Keller's moral rigor, his insistence on the ineluctability of experience in its relentless temporal flow, separates his novel from so many of the texts discussed here. Yet I think it would be wrong to see *Green Henry* as a work that breaks with the Bildungsroman tradition. In the first place, we have obvious links with the tradition: the young hero as a man searching for a fuller realization of himself than that vouchsafed by the world in which he grows up; the encounter with two different modes of erotic experience in the contrasting figures of Anna and Judith; hints of the characteristic providentiality of Bildungsroman plot in the meeting with Dortchen and her uncle and in the return of Judith at the end. Most important, we have the narrative perspective which I highlighted above. The recollecting self celebrates precisely that modest human wholeness that is the interaction of world and self, of facts and imaginative allegiance. The novel intimates, in other words, that the prose of narrow circumstances can interlock with the poetry of the individual imagination, that human reality is an existential category in which the limited world of practical affairs can come alive with inward validation. Keller is not the philistine apologist of a banal status quo. As narrator he highlights what his hero fails to recognize: the richness and poetry immanent in the real. Heinrich's quest for a fulfilling life leads him to supplant the real by the imaginative, to esteem potentiality above actuality. Keller's moral astringency illuminates the flaws for what they are, insisting that Heinrich pay the price for disregarding external reality, that is, that he condemn himself increasingly to a lifeless existence. In one sense, we can see Keller's novel as a critical debate with a novel tradition that inclines to cherish the potential rather than the actual, inwardness

rather than outward self-realization, that all too frequently operates with a highly tentative relationship to
facts, deeds, and the practicalities of human interaction.
But in another sense, we must recognize that Keller's
novel is a debate conducted from within that tradition.
What the narrator affirms is not simply the joyless credo
of no-nonsense hard work. Rather, it is that the world,
if underwritten by the allegiance of the individual in all
his inwardness, becomes the vessel for a wholeness that
is the lifeblood not only of right living but also of art.
Artistic and moral validation go hand in hand. Thereby,
I would suggest, Keller's novel partakes of that tentative
teleology inherent in the Bildungsroman tradition. The
protagonist may lose his way, but the novel itself—
thanks to its informing narrative presence—does not.
The characteristic tension between the *Nacheinander* of
plot and the *Nebeneinander* of human potential may become a complete dualism in Heinrich's actual experience, but that tension is an artistically sustained presence in *Green Henry* because of Keller's interlocking of
experiencing and narrating self.

══ VI ══
Mann:
The Magic Mountain
(1924)*

Critical discussion of *The Magic Mountain* continues with
unabated energy. Despite the multiplicity of diverging
viewpoints and approaches, however, there is still an
approximate consensus of opinion about the function of
the hero, Hans Castorp, and about the thematic import
of the experiences he undergoes in the rarefied air of
the sanatorium world.[1] This consensus could be summarized as follows: Hans Castorp, a simple, somewhat
mediocre young man leaves the world of good Hamburg society to which he belongs and travels to Davos in
order to visit his cousin Joachim, who is a patient in the
Berghof sanatorium. His short visit turns into a seven-
year sojourn when it is discovered that he himself is suffering from tuberculosis. In the hermetic, feverish atmosphere of the enchanted mountain the ordinary stuff
of which Hans Castorp is made undergoes a heightening and enhancing process that makes him capable of
adventures in sensual, moral, and intellectual spheres
he would never have dreamed of in the flatland. Narratively, this process is intimated through Castorp's contact with various characters who are in effect exponents,
representatives, emissaries from domains of the spirit.

---

* This chapter is a reworked version of my paper, "The Story and
the Hero: A Study of Thomas Mann's *Der Zauberberg*," DVLG, 46
(1972), 359ff.

[1] For a full discussion of the relevant literature see Jürgen Scharfschwerdt, *Thomas Mann und der deutsche Bildungsroman* (Stuttgart,
1967), esp. 114-15. Scharfschwerdt himself argues that in the first half
of the novel Hans Castorp does undergo a certain personal development, whereas the second half is more abstract, with the hero being
used as a cipher for the author's reflections on *Bildung*.

The macabre adventures through which Hans Castorp passes are a pedagogic instrument, used to accomplish the heightening and enhancement of the hero to a point far beyond his original competence. And pedagogically, the Magic Mountain experience works. Castorp learns to overcome his inborn attraction to death and arrives at an understanding of humanity that does not simply ignore death nor scorn the dark, mysterious side of life. He takes account of death, but without letting it gain control of his mind. It is this notion of disease, and of death as a necessary route to knowledge, health, and life, that makes *The Magic Mountain* a novel of initiation. Like the traditional seeker after the Grail, Hans Castorp has to undergo various terrible ordeals before he may approach his goal. And that goal, the Grail of his quest, is to be found in the chapter "Snow," where, lost in perilous heights, he dreams his dream of humanity. If he does not find the Grail, yet he divines it in his deathly dream before he is snatched downward from his heights into the European catastrophe.

That most Mann critics would agree on this kind of outline of the basic theme of *The Magic Mountain* is perhaps hardly surprising, because the foregoing summary of the novel's thematic purpose is taken, for the greater part word for word, from Thomas Mann himself, from his paper, "The Making of *The Magic Mountain*," a lecture given in the United States and reprinted at the end of the Lowe-Porter translation.[2] In my view, however, Mann's own remarks on his novel capture only one part of the total meaning of the work. *The Magic Mountain* is much more complex and differentiated than this simple summary of Hans Castorp's development suggests. I might here summarize my rea-

[2] Mann, *The Magic Mountain*, trans. H. Lowe-Porter (New York, 1965), 719-29. I have drawn on the Lowe-Porter translation in my rendering of the German quotations, but I have on occasion modified her version where I felt this was appropriate.

sons for believing that this outline of Hans Castorp's function is misleading. There are four aspects which trouble me, and none more so than the pedagogic notion that the hero develops in the course of the novel to a "point far beyond his original competence."[3] In the first place, what kind of competence is involved here? Intellectual, imaginative, moral competence? Furthermore, do the last three chapters or so of the novel show us a hero who is manifestly in possession of certain values which he did not have at the beginning? My second objection concerns the whole question of *The Magic Mountain* as a novel of initiation, as a novel with a Grail. I can see that there are insight moments in the novel, moments when Hans Castorp perceives some aspect or aspects of the human condition. Yet, each time, the insight moment is forgotten, is relativized by what follows it. And this fact leads me to question whether there is an explicit value center to Mann's novel. If such a center does exist, then it may indeed be the "Snow" chapter. But does Hans Castorp's dream vision of the Sun People function as the climactic wisdom of this massive novel? Does the hero's vision stand up intellectually and stylistically within the context of the novel? My final objection concerns the structure of the novel. If the snow vision does stand up, why does it not come nearer to the end of the novel? It is significant in this context to note that Mann's remarks about the "Snow" chapter being the Grail of the novel operate with a misleading time scale. He writes that Hans Castorp "divines [the Grail] in his deathly dream, before he is snatched downward from his heights into the European catastrophe."[4] In fact, however, some two hundred pages follow the "Snow" chapter, and in these pages one of the most crucial characters of the whole novel makes his appearance: Mynheer Peeperkorn. It is noteworthy that two

---

[3] Ibid., 726. [4] Ibid., 729.

recent publications have concerned themselves specifically with the impact Peeperkorn makes on Hans Castorp, and both have suggested that the appearance of
Peeperkorn at this late stage of the novel serves to relativize much of what precedes his arrival at the Berghof
sanatorium.[5]

In order to clarify the remarkable elusiveness of the
hero's development in *The Magic Mountain* it is necessary to examine in some detail those insight points that
do occur in the course of Hans Castorp's seven years
spent in the sanatorium. One aspect should be stressed
at the outset: Hans Castorp is vouchsafed these moments of insight as a result of his confrontation with a
quite specific world, with the world of extremes that is
the Berghof. The comment the narrator makes about
Frau Ziemssen's attempt to moderate the hilarity of the
cousins when they are reunited is pertinent here: "It
was essentially for reasons of propriety that she had
wanted to introduce a little moderate seriousness, not
knowing that precisely the moderate, the middle way
was completely unknown here and only a choice between extremes was offered" (531).[6]

The sense in which the sanatorium represents a world
of extremes is suggested at several points in the novel: it
is a world that makes the intellectual more purely intellectual (that is, cerebral) in that there are no everyday
practicalities to relativize the articulation of certain intel-

---

[5] J. G. Brennan, "Heard and Unheard Speech in *The Magic Mountain*," *Novel*, 3 (1970), 129-38, and Winfried Kudszus, "Peeperkorns
Lieblingsjünger," *Wirkendes Wort*, 20 (1970), 321-30. I disagree, however, with both critics in their attempt to create a specific value center
for the novel. See Herbert Lehnert's argument about the lack of *Bil-
dungsergebnis* ("Hans Castorp's Vision," *Rice University Studies*, 47
[1960], 1-37). See also Herman Weigand's observation that Castorp's
quest is not only for *Erkenntnis* but also for *Erlebnis* (*The Magic Mountain* [Chapel Hill, 1964], 156).

[6] References throughout are to Thomas Mann, *Der Zauberberg*
(Frankfurt: Fischer-Bücherei, 1967).

lectual positions; it is also a world that makes the physical more purely physical in that sickness invites acquiescence in the body's complete domination of the human personality. The implications of the extreme nature of the Berghof world are important when one examines that process of interaction between Hans Castorp and the Berghof which yields the insight moments. For that interaction process is the substance of the story that the novel tells.

The Hans Castorp who arrives at the Berghof may be a mediocre young man, as the narrator tells us, but his mediocrity is not without its problematic aspects. His background and lineage are shot through with contradictions. He is a young man who has reverence for the "baptismal bowl," for the respectable continuity of bourgeois tradition. Embedded in this tradition, however, is a death experience, an experience intrinsically ambiguous. Death is part of the family tradition; it is something dignified and mysterious, something shrouded in due ceremony. At the same time, it is known to be nothing more than a crude process of physical disintegration. Both aspects find a response in Hans Castorp, just as in school he both recognizes the practical obligation to get on and also develops a taste for "the limitless advantages of shame" (87). In this sense Castorp is a being poised between contradictions, a problem child of life. From the warring opposites that operate within him he also gains symbolical stature: as a young German, as a figure representing the German spirit poised between East and West, between an ethos of military discipline and order on the one hand, and surrender to imaginative excesses that obliterate all claims of practical social living on the other.

The interaction of Hans Castorp, in all his problematic mediocrity, with the Berghof world of extremes is the subject matter of *The Magic Mountain*. A complex of thematic strands interweave to form the texture of the novel as a whole. And the strands constantly interact in the sense that they comment on and relativize each other. At crucial points along the plot thread the strands emerge and constitute a focus, a moment of insight, a new understanding for Castorp. Common to these focus points is the notion of man as a being greater than any of the dualisms his reflective faculty perceives. And yet Hans Castorp forgets the insight he has gained, the focus point fades, the themes become submerged in the general texture—only to reappear elsewhere.

I wish to comment in detail on four of these focus points. The first concerns Hans Castorp and medicine. Its explicit formulation is to be found in the chapter "Researches," where Castorp, largely under the impetus of a recent conversation with Hofrat Behrens, devotes his attention to the study of medical textbooks. In their conversation Castorp had learned that the life process is chemically identical with the dying process (oxidation). The only difference is that in life the organic form is preserved and constantly renews itself. This chemical fact, Castorp reflects, is a precondition of man's being, and of his entire reflective, analytical, speculative capacity:

> Consciousness of oneself was therefore a function of matter organized into living cells, and in the higher species this function turned against its own organism, became a striving to penetrate and explain the phenomenon which brought it into being, a hopeful yet doomed striving of life for self-knowledge, nature beating at the doors of its own being, and ultimately all in vain, as nature cannot dissolve into perfect self-knowledge, as life cannot eavesdrop on its own workings. (291)

Insight, intellectual understanding, is a function of the material constitution of man and can therefore never fully understand the process of which it is a part because it cannot stand outside the context of its own functioning. This crucial notion relativizes much of

Naphta's and Settembrini's endless debates about spirit and matter. It reveals their intellectualism as a process of bloodless cerebration, as operating with the false postulation of the spirit of man, his self-awareness, as something over against and contemplatively separate from his material selfhood. Furthermore, this notion questions the whole nature of human insight in that it suggests the incompleteness of any intellectual construct that claims to know and understand life. Hence, it is the purpose of this particular moment of insight that Hans Castorp be made to question how much can be learned from moments of reflective analysis.

The second focus point involves Castorp and the notion of form. Its explicit center is the chapter "Dance of Death," where Castorp decides to take an interest in the dying patients in the sanatorium. The purpose behind his visits is to offer formal expressions of sympathy and condolence. In the chapter that depicts the death of Joachim the point is made that this capacity for compassion linked with formal observances of decency and decorum distinguishes man from animals, that is, man is able to answer death by form and therein expresses his humanity. The theme of form is something we have already encountered in the "medical" focus point: form is that which distinguishes living from dying. Man's capacity for giving form to experience is what makes him truly human. Form is also seen as central to the medical profession: doctors formalize by means of Latinate categorizations the multifarious possibilities of sickness. In this sense they answer the process of dissolution, decay, and loss of form by strict formality. Form, Castorp comes to realize, is at the heart of any humane morality, for human dignity resides in the ability to know of the abyss and to answer it with form, with ceremony and observances (a notion inherent in Castorp's reverence for the "baptismal bowl"). Form, then, represents control and order; it is purposive, it is morally good.

But, as with the previous focus point, this moment of

insight too cannot simply be possessed as a stable intimation of abiding value. Once glimpsed, it is to be forgotten. The theme of form finds its own relativization in
the notion of Spanish court etiquette (Castorp's references to *Don Carlos*), which emerges as both the ultimate
expression of human dignity and willpower, and also as
a constriction of life, a schematization of human behavior to the point of lifelessness. This relativization of the
theme of form becomes explicit in the introduction to
the next thematic crystallization point, the "Snow"
chapter: as Hans Castorp blunders through the swirling
snowflakes he reflects that the snowflake in its total
formal perfection represents a *deathly* perfection, an
order to which all dynamic and flux has been sacrificed.

The "Snow" chapter begins with a journey into obliterating death, a journey that involves a process of *un-
kommen* (the etymological pun—"to come in a circle"
and "to die"—is made explicit). And yet this journey to
the edge of the abyss yields a dream of perfect humanity, of the Sun People, who live a life of sensuous beauty
and ordered, serene social intercourse, while yet knowing of the dark, mysterious horrors embedded in the
very heart of life. Before commenting on the substance
of this dream image of human wholeness and perfection, it is, I think, appropriate to review the conclusions
that Hans Castorp draws from it. There can be no doubt
that these conclusions are important, not only to Castorp himself—he desperately tries to hammer them into
his brain—but also to the narrator, who resorts to italics
in order to emphasize the importance of the insights
gained.

Castorp concludes that man truly is the problem child
of life because of the inescapable ambiguity of his situation, an ambiguity that informs even the values by
which he seeks to live. There is no one answer to life's
complexities because there are no one-dimensional,
abiding certainties. This leads Castorp to reject both

Naphta and Settembrini as empty talkers, as windbags, as false propounders of easy doctrines. Their falsity resides in the exclusive extremism of their respective positions, for as Castorp comes to realize, so many polar opposites are not necessarily antagonists. Rather, they are subsumable under a meaningful, coherent, and humane wholeness. This is the center of Castorp's insight: because man's being houses and encompasses multiple dualisms, his being is greater than all the dualisms and contradictions which his reflective faculty so relentlessly perceives. Here we are in effect concerned with a reworking of the "medical" insight: man is in danger of postulating a free-floating mind separate from the physical organism whose existence and functioning is a precondition of his thinking at all. To talk of a dualism between matter and spirit is therefore cerebral nonsense; the mind needs the body in order to be able to formulate its denial of and withdrawal from the body. The lesson to be learned, then, is love of man, love of that process—life—which enables him to know himself to the extent that he does, and above all, love of that process which makes him so much more of a totality than he is ever able to perceive intellectually. This is the italicized message of the "Snow" chapter: *"for the sake of goodness and love man should not allow death to take charge of his thoughts"* (523). It would seem, then, that the "Snow" chapter is a point of climactic insight within the novel. But intellectually, it says no more than the other focus points. It reaches the same conclusion, a conclusion which is then, as we are quite explicitly told, forgotten by Hans Castorp. In other words, it is as valid as the other focus points, no more and no less.

What distinguishes this section from all the other insight points, however, is that the moment of insight is not simply formulated discursively and stated in conceptual terms, but is also made concrete in an image of human existence and activity, the Sun People. It is this concretization that I find questionable. In my view, the dream sequence is overwritten to the point of being a melodramatic scenario.[7] It is in part a euphoric wish-dream emanating from the mind of a young man lost in a blizzard. The vision is not without touches of irony, as when the witches hurl obscenities at Castorp in his native Hamburg dialect. The dream derives from the hero's present longing for warmth and sunlight, from his craving for an image of human wholeness and integration as opposed to the partial and extreme figures of the Berghof. But whether the Sun People are an intellectually satisfying embodiment of this wholeness seems to me questionable. Hans Castorp's fevered brain attempts to construct an image which can express such wholeness in visible and concrete terms. The Sun People on the beach know of the horror of the human sacrifice—the boy's gaze darkens as his eyes alight on the temple—but they make no attempt to halt the monstrousness of the human sacrifice. They simply acquiesce in the fact that it is, and thereby, surely, they lay themselves open to the charge of smugness and callousness.

It is, then, the dream image which I find stylistically and intellectually questionable. The conclusions that Hans Castorp draws—which the narrator describes as a continuation of the dream "no longer in images, but in thoughts, although for all that no less venturesome and confused" (521)—are acceptable in that they represent, as elsewhere in the novel, a grappling on the conceptual level with the antinomies that make up existence, and with the human totality under which they are ultimately subsumable. Yet this insight fades like all the others.

The fourth insight point centers upon the theme of love. The theme of course appears in a variety of guises throughout the novel, but it finds its focus—surpris-

---

[7] See Scharfschwerdt, *Mann und der deutsche Bildungsroman*, 142, where similar objections are voiced.

ingly perhaps, but importantly in my view—not with
reference to Hans Castorp's love for another human being, but rather in the context of his love for a human
construct, for a song, the "Lindenbaum." The song itself, we are told, has simple strength and energy, a
folksy sturdiness, but it knows of death. The return for
which it longs is the return to a simple state, return to a
peace that obliterates everything, all sorrow, all joy, all
individuation, the peace of death. Castorp's love for this
intrinsically ambiguous song is equal to and aware of
the ambiguity of the thing loved. His love encompasses
detachment and attraction, passionate assent and critical distance; it is self-aware, yet profound. The narrator
explicitly describes the nature of Hans Castorp's love,
that it is an eros deeply ironic and self-critical:

> Is one to believe that our simple hero after so and so
> many years a hermetic-pedagogic enhancement has
> penetrated sufficiently deeply into spiritual matters
> in order to be *aware* of the significance of his love
> and of its object. We assert and tell that he was. The
> song meant a great deal to him, a whole world, in-
> deed a world which he perforce loved, otherwise he
> could not have been so infatuated with its repre-
> sentative symbol. We know what we are saying
> when we—perhaps somewhat obscurely—add that
> his fate would have shaped itself very differently if
> his heart had not been excessively responsive to the
> charms of that emotional world, of that general
> spiritual attitude which the song summarized in its
> heartfelt, mysterious way. But precisely this fate
> had brought with it enhancements, adventures, in-
> sights, had caused reflective difficulties within him,
> which had made him capable of perceptive criticism
> of this world, of this its admittedly admirable sym-
> bol, of this his love—such that all three became the
> object of moral scruple. (689)

And yet, here again the moment of insight is taken back, is relativized, as Castorp goes on to falsify his insight, his love. In the passage I have just quoted the narrator asserts the clarity—and the rightness—of Hans Castorp's perception. But our hero cannot leave it at that:

Hans Castorp's thoughts or intuitive half-thoughts flew high as he sat in night and loneliness in front of his silent musical sarcophagus. They flew higher than his reason could go, they were alchemistically enhanced thoughts. Oh it was powerful this magic of the soul. We all were its sons and we could achieve mighty things on earth by serving it. . . . But its best son might be whosoever in self-transcendence consumed his own life and died, on his lips the new word of love which he could not yet utter. It was so worth dying for, this magic song! But he who died for it, did not actually die for it anymore—he was a hero insofar as he died for the new, for the new word of love, of the future in his heart. (691)

This is a passionate and rhetorical passage. In it, Hans Castorp dreams of a love beyond, outside this his present love for the "Lindenbaum." He postulates a distant, future realm in which a truly regenerate love will be possible, some mystical future which promises release from present ambiguity. But this is false reasoning. Because Hans Castorp can apprehend the contradictions at work within his own person he is a being greater than those contradictions. The synthesis is there already, now, in the fact of his being, in the differentiated love of which it is capable. And yet it is a synthesis, a totality, rarely known for what it is because it can only be glimpsed and then forgotten. It does not show itself in a sustained and cumulative revelatory process to the eager mind of the self-examining Castorp. Hence, that very process of examination leads Hans Castorp to pro-

ject his longing for present wholeness onto some tem-
porally distant mode of fulfillment. He postulates a time
sequence, a direction, that will in the future yield synthesis. And the future of which he dreams is, typically,
a speculative and imaginative construct, a future beyond the present ambiguity of his situation, a future
that promises synthesis by evasion, by obliterating the
mode of being that yields the antinomies that cry out for
synthesis.

Such musings on Hans Castorp's part are described
as "alchemistically enhanced." They represent the point
at which his capacity for self-examination, which is
heightened by the extreme world of the Berghof, suc-
cumbs to the rarefied atmosphere of the sanatorium, to
the luxury of juggling endlessly with speculative cere-
bralities. This, then, is the value and the danger of the
hermetic pedagogy to which Hans Castorp is exposed.
The process of alchemistic enhancing has its value: it intensifies and crystallizes certain aspects of Hans Castorp's being; it makes him aware of what he is. But the
awareness is always questioned by what goes before
and what comes after, and such awareness as Castorp
gains emerges briefly, only to be forgotten, or falsified,
or relativized almost as soon as it has appeared. This
rhythmic pattern is central to the novel, to the meaning
it yields, and to the question of how far and in what way
Hans Castorp develops, if he develops at all. There
would seem to be considerable evidence for a conclusion that Castorp does not develop. One thinks particularly of the remarks with which the narrator opens and
closes his story: the story is worth telling for its own
sake and not on account of the hero, who is a simple but
engaging young man, although, as it is *his* story and no
one else's, he must be entitled to some credit for his participation. What does one make of such remarks, of the
constant stress on our hero's *Mittelmässigkeit* (mediocrity)?

Quite obviously, Hans Castorp is the focus of the

novel in the simple sense that his presence at the Berghof is the precise precondition of the plot. If we follow the plot thread through the novel, we find that there are certain points along that sequence of events, related in chronological order, where the whole process yields purpose and values are revealed. This is, of course, what we traditionally expect of plot: events in sequence that coalesce to yield meaning. As I have suggested in my discussion of four of the thematic focus points, we do encounter moments in the plot that are unmistakably value heavy. All these moments of insight are associated with Hans Castorp. The conceptualizations of meaning are his or are specifically imputed to him by the narrator. It is therefore very tempting to assume that Castorp derives an abiding insight from these experiences. Oddly enough, however, he seems to forget them.

Perhaps one can best illuminate this elusive quality about the hero's progression through the novel by constructing a different ending. *The Magic Mountain* would be a very different novel if after the "Snow" chapter Hans Castorp left the sanatorium of his own accord and returned to the plains in order to become a doctor (in terms of cultural tradition, a very respectable conclusion; one thinks of Goethe's *Wilhelm Meister's Travels*), or if the closing chapter showed him as a member of a field hospital, surrounded by bursting shells, with little chance of survival, but with the narratively intimated certainty that the values which he has learned and which he is enacting in his work will outlive him. I cannot help but feel that this is the kind of conclusion many people would have wished Thomas Mann to reach. But emphatically he did not. In other words, it seems to me questionable whether Hans Castorp develops in the traditional sense in which we understand a novel hero's development, that is, learning consistently and cumulatively from his experience to the point where he can then enact the values he has acquired. Hans Castorp is and remains "mittelmässig," mediocre, or perhaps more accurately, undistinguished by any dominant characteristic, propensity, or quality. Therein, of course, resides his crucial importance. When Hans Castorp arrives at the Berghof, all the experiences and values he meets are present implicitly, latently within him (just as, for example, the Clawdia experience is already inherent in his being, as we know from his boyhood infatuation with Pribislav Hippe). What the Berghof does is to confront him with these values and experiences in extreme, heightened form. It intensifies an aspect of his being by confronting him with the explicit articulation of that aspect. But Hans Castorp himself is and remains "mittelmässig"; he is and remains the "Mittel-mass," the middle way, in which all the extremes potentially are present.[8] In this sense one can in part see Castorp as a catalyst: his presence forces the interaction, confrontation, and, ultimately, relativization of those values and attitudes which find their exclusive and extreme exponents in the rarefied air of the Berghof sanatorium. But like any catalyst, Castorp himself remains unchanged. Of course, Hans Castorp is a special kind of catalyst: he is a human being, and the values which interact so busily around him are all present and coexistent within him in a way that is not true of any of the other characters in the novel. Hence the paradox with which Mann begins and ends his novel: the story matters more than Castorp himself; the interaction of values matters. But without Castorp's presence the interaction would not take place in the explicit and overt way that it does. And without his presence the interdependence of these values, their

[8] The distinction I have in mind here is akin to that drawn by Hans Mayer between Castorp as an open possibility and the other characters as "extreme positions" (*Thomas Mann: Werke und Entwicklung* [Berlin, 1950], 129-30).

coexistence as a corpus of human possibilities of which no one constellation automatically excludes the others, would not reveal itself. Hence, central to the meaning of the four focus points I have discussed is that Hans Castorp should forget the insight he has gained. Any insight into the wholeness of man is immediately relativized by the fact that this moment of insight represents the luxury of a contemplative relationship to experience. The moment of insight cannot be prolonged because it is the nature of the insight that the intellect, the faculty for conceptualizing experience, is only part of man and part of his experience. It may briefly apprehend the whole truth, but it cannot *be* the whole truth because the whole truth is a totally interacting dynamic. Any attempt to prolong the moment of insight into a serenely contemplative relationship to experience falsifies the insight and leads to a simple indulgence in cerebralizings about life.

It is this notion of human wholeness that *The Magic Mountain*, in my view, is concerned to intimate. It accounts for the curiously dominant stature which Hans Castorp in all his indeterminateness acquires. But Castorp's dominance can only be implied. It defies concrete enactment and depiction for reasons which are important for an understanding of Mann's whole relationship to the novel form. To these reasons I want to return later. Suffice it to say at this stage that there is no one event, no one situation, no one human confrontation that functions as the novel's explicit value center. In this belief I find myself at variance with most Thomas Mann critics, even with those who have questioned the validity of the Sun People vision in "Snow."[9] Indeed, it

---

[9] See n. 5 above. I would also question the conclusions reached by Scharfschwerdt and Theodore Ziolkowski (see his *Dimensions of the Modern Novel* [Princeton, 1969]), which lay great weight on the narrative voice as the source of coherence and value in the novel. In my view, even the narrator's perspective is not the value center of the novel.

seems to me central to the novel's meaning that there can be no concretization of the wholeness of humanity that transcends all dualisms. The one attempt at explicit depiction and embodiment of this wholeness leads to the dream sequence in "Snow." In other words, we are concerned with a totality that can only be focused conceptually—this is what happens at the moments of insight. But the insights are discursive *statements* concerning the nature of this wholeness, they do not embody it in a concrete image. Similarly, none of the characters whom Castorp meets during his stay at the Berghof is allowed to represent the total interacting complexity of man's being. The "medical" theme does not find its explicit enactment in Krokowski or Behrens; the "form" theme is not concretized by the figure of Joachim; the "love" theme is not embodied in the person of Frau Chauchat. Nor indeed does Peeperkorn stand for the sum total of life's experience. The nearest we get to an image of this sum total (and with it to the value center of the novel) is the implicit dominance of Hans Castorp himself. The reason why this dominance is implicit rather than explicit, suggested rather than stated, lies above all in the function of the narrative voice.

Throughout *The Magic Mountain* one is aware of the narrator's lofty, pedagogically patronizing relationship to the main character. The tone is all important because it suggests that the narrator is part of the Berghof world. He is, as Theodore Ziolkowski aptly puts it, "tied to the locale; he is the *genius loci*."[10] It is interesting to note that at the end of the novel, when the narrator bids farewell to his main character, his voice sounds like Settembrini's, and he even repeats the latter's gesture of touching the corner of his eye with his finger tip. The narrator's voice is located in and works through a world of extremes. It verbalizes these extremes with the irony appropriate to such extremes, thereby intimating both

---

[10] Ziolkowski, *Dimensions of the Modern Novel*, 95.

the excitement and the human questionableness of the hermetic pedagogy of the Berghof world. It implicitly suggests the curious richness of the indeterminate figure of Hans Castorp, a richness that derives from the unutterable complexity of life in all its contradictions, so much richer than the other characters—ultimately, so much more a totality than the narrative voice can say.

In the last sentence of the novel the narrator asks whether love will one day rise from the insane holocaust of the war. His plea reminds us of Hans Castorp's "alchemistically enhanced" thoughts at the end of the "Lindenbaum" section. There Castorp postulated some removed future, some new world of love, as an image of a distant totality for which man strives. But these thoughts were a falsity, just as the narrator's question is a falsity. The love of which the pedagogically heightened Hans Castorp and the pedagogic narrator speak is, like man himself, the father and child of contradictions. It is the sum total of life experience, a totality that can never be possessed in terms of a specific turning point within a linear time sequence. Hence, the narrator's question at the end of the novel, a question that operates within a linear time scale—"will love ever arise?" (757)—is relativized by the whole novel. Love will not come at some time. It is *now* in life, unsayable, intimated through a narrative irony, through an unspoken relationship to the main character that ultimately ironizes its own presence as traditional narrator, as spinner of the plot thread, as "intoning wizard of the imperfect" (5).

The narrative voice tells a story in time sequence. In order to do this it refracts life through the prism of the hero's confrontation with the Berghof world into some of its component values, concepts, ideologies, and attitudes. The novel can narrate the temporal sequence within which these strands of being appear, but the totality of Hans Castorp's "mediocrity" cannot be narrated as such because it is not straightforwardly realizable in plot, in linear concretization. The unexceptional indeterminateness of Hans Castorp cannot say its own sum total, it can only *be* it. Thus the narrative voice is imprisoned within its own function as reporter of events in chronological sequence. The only way out of this constriction is irony and the intimation through irony that what can be said is only a small part of what needs to be said. This ironic intimation, this narrative that questions its own function as novel narrative, is the only way of making the spark of meaning jump the gap between language and silence.

Of course, the process of ironic intimation also involves plot. Obviously, *The Magic Mountain* does have a plot thread, a chain of events arranged in the *Nacheinander* of linear time sequence. Yet the relationship between the narrative voice and the person of the hero is not the only feature of the novel's construction and theme that relativizes the validity of the traditional presuppositions of plot. For example, the recurring routine of the Berghof, its hermetic quality, sealed off from time like preserves in a jar (Hans Castorp's image), the whole theme of time, of time as subjective perception, of time as its own dimension, as a continuum rather than a transparent vessel for containing and pigeonholing human activities—these and many other aspects contribute to the process. They find ample discursive treatment in the novel itself, and critics have analyzed them fully.[11]

In the sense that *The Magic Mountain* has a *Nacheinander* but is centrally concerned with a *Nebeneinander*, with a complex coexistence of possibilities, with the value-heavy *nunc stans* of Hans Castorp's being, it is a novel which questions what can be said by the traditional novel form of narrative sequence. *The Magic Mountain* is, then, very much part of that cardinal experience of the

[11] See for example Ulrich Karthaus, "*Der Zauberberg*—ein Zeitroman," *DVLG*, 44 (1970), 269ff.

modern novel which Theodor W. Adorno has aphoristi-
cally summarized: "It is no longer possible to tell a
story, while the novel form demands story telling."[12]
One must ask, however, why so many major writers of
the twentieth century, Mann included, have not taken
the final step of dissolving the narrative sequence altogether, why many novels cling tenaciously to some
sort of plot, if only in order to parody it. Perhaps the
reason for this remarkably persistent residue of events
in time sequence is that, whatever happens, man is
obliged to live out his life, and to conceive of it, within
the linear temporality of practical existence. He may not
be able to affirm this sequence, to see it as in any way
expressing that which is valid, important, or necessary,
but like it or not, he is still caught up in this mode of
existence. It is central to the honesty of *The Magic
Mountain* that Hans Castorp is, in the last resort, power-
less. The crucial decisions as to what happens with his
life are not his: world history decides for him. Mann
carefully documents the growing seediness of the Berghof; the hysteria enveloping the plains is felt even in the
Magic Mountain. In the last analysis, Hans Castorp's
complexity means nothing when he is sucked into the
worldwide death feast. That the problem child of life
ends up as cannon fodder gives *The Magic Mountain* a
tragic resonance.

It is by now a truism in discussion of *The Magic Mountain* to describe it as a parodistic Bildungsroman. There
are two immediate senses in which the parody is manifest: first, the real social world which Hans Castorp en-
ters at the end of the novel is a chaotic and violent confusion which simply does not allow him to see his way
clear to a fulfilling relationship with human society; second, the educative environment bears no relationship to
the common realm of ordinary human encounters and

[12] Adorno, "Standort des Erzählers im zeitgenössischen Roman,"
in *Noten zur Literatur*, 1 (Frankfurt, 1968), 61.

interaction but is rather the "hermetic" and sick world of the sanatorium. The relationship to the Bildungsroman is admittedly parodistic, but there is more to it than this. *The Magic Mountain* involves not simply an exploration of the tradition and a critique of it, but also a precarious reinstatement of it. It is this latter aspect which deserves special attention, the sense in which Mann's novel in part fulfills the genre because it illuminates aspects of it which were always more tentative and problematic than traditional literary history has allowed. The question of plot is an obvious example of what I mean. The traditional Bildungsroman at one level always tends to question the linear time sequence of narrative, that is, the characters the hero meets exist for the most part in order to bring out strands within his being. This accounts for the curious lack of experiential finality in the Bildungsroman: one rarely has the sense of an irrevocable interaction between the hero and the world in which he moves. This tentative relationship to experience, this lack of immediacy in the hero's confrontation with events, goes back a long way. As Schiller wrote to Goethe in 1796:

> Wilhelm Meister is of course the most necessary, but not the most important person: precisely that is one of the peculiarities of your novel that it neither has nor needs such a most important person. *To* him and *around* him everything happens, but not essentially *for his sake.* Because the things around him represent and express energies and he embodies educability, he has to stand in quite a different relationship to the other characters from that which the hero in other novels has. [13]

The paradox Schiller recognized is the same paradox with which Mann opens and closes his novel: the story

[13] *Hamburger Ausgabe*, VIII, 550.

is told for its own sake, not for the hero's, because the hero is not a clearly defined character, he is not a "personality" in the accepted sense of the term. Yet the hero is the precondition of the story; everything that happens in fact befalls *him*.

In effect, the hero both has and does not have a story. This is the characteristic tension of the Bildungsroman to which I have so often referred, that between the *Nacheinander* of plot and the *Nebeneinander* of human potentiality and wholeness. Both *Wilhelm Meister's Apprenticeship* and *The Magic Mountain* enact this tension: the "Snow" vision as a discursive perception of human wholeness is as surely relativized by the ongoing flow of events as is the Society of the Tower in *Wilhelm Meister*. In my view, Mann's novel, like all sophisticated parody, represents a last-ditch fulfillment—and illumination—of the thing it parodies.

T. J. Reed has shown how Mann's whole conception of *The Magic Mountain* changed in the course of its composition.[14] Mann began work on the project in 1913, at which time it was intended as a humorous companion piece to *Death in Venice*. But the material grew in resonance as Mann, under the pressure of the early months of the war, found that "its figures and story irresistibly became . . . representative of the issues he believed the war was about."[15] In other words, "if he had been able to complete the novel during the war, it would certainly have been a fictional expression of his Romantic anti-westernism."[16] But Mann was not able to finish the novel during the war years. The completed version, which did not appear until 1924, bears the imprint of his decisive change of mind and heart. For he came to abjure the unpolitical attitudes of German conservatism

[14] Reed, *Thomas Mann: The Uses of Tradition* (Oxford, 1974), 226ff., and "Thomas Mann: The Writer as Historian of his Time," *Modern Language Review*, 71 (1976), 82ff.

[15] Reed, "Mann as Historian," 85.   [16] Ibid., 86.

and to plead for a commitment to practical affairs, to politics, to parliamentary democracy. For Reed, the genesis of *The Magic Mountain* shows a process of growth and education undergone by the author; hence Mann "himself had completed the education which *The Magic Mountain* relates. This is how the Bildungsroman became possible, and necessary."[17] Clearly, on numerous points Reed is right. However, I think that Mann's employment of the Bildungsroman genre should be seen less as an announcement of an unambiguously didactic intention than as a precise engagement with a German tradition to which, under the impact of political events, his allegiance had become ever more critical. One can see this dual relationship with particular clarity in the last few pages of the novel. We are told that Hans Castorp had "allowed himself, to be sure, to dream this and that about the spiritual shadows of things in his usual reflective way, but had paid no attention to the things themselves—in fact out of the arrogant propensity to take shadows for things, but to see in things merely shadows . . . " (750). This sounds like a very thoroughgoing repudiation of that complex inwardness which the Bildungsroman is so often concerned both to explore and to validate. It would seem, then, that the novel's end takes back all that precedes it, that the massively (and lovingly) chronicled debate about human values, with its omnipresent concern for the wholeness of man, amounts in the last resort to nothing in a world where the mud of the Somme has the last word for a whole European generation.

Yet—and not surprisingly when one is concerned with something from Thomas Mann's pen—the issues are not so simple. The narrator does indeed make his devastating criticism of Castorp's "arrogance" (and, by implication, of the arrogance of the fastidiously unpolit-

[17] Reed, *Thomas Mann*, 244.

ical German tradition), but then immediately goes on to qualify his strictures: "out of the arrogant propensity to take shadows for things, but to see in things only shadows—for which one should not scold him too harshly, since the relationship between the two has not been finally settled" (750). So perhaps, in spite of the irrevocable inroads made by world history into the fastness of Hans Castorp's retreat in the Berghof, there is after all a distinction and value to that process which this novel, like all Bildungsromane, chronicles. The *Nacheinander* of practical and physical existence is the ultimate arbiter of an individual life, but the *Nebeneinander* of human inwardness is the source of human complexity and interest. Outwardly, Hans Castorp is swallowed up without trace; inwardly, he has the distinction of trying to know himself more strenuously than the practical world of the flatlands would ever have permitted. This is Thomas Mann's grudging—and in its grudgingness, wonderfully right—engagement with the Bildungsroman tradition.

= VII =
Hesse:
The Glass Bead Game
(1943)

Hermann Hesse's *The Glass Bead Game* closes with a number of short poems and stories which apparently constitute Josef Knecht's posthumous writings. The three stories, or *Lebensläufe* (biographies), derive directly from the educative process which Knecht has undergone (all Castalian students are required, as part of their training, to compose such fictional lives). Knecht's stories all concern a protagonist who ultimately finds insight into the right way of life, thereby attaining that integrity of purpose and being which he seeks. The final story tells of a young prince who comes to realize that all experience is vanity, that the path to truth and peace proceeds through contemplation, through acquiring the skills of the Yogi. When Prince Dasa begins this life of spiritual service, "There is no more to be told about Dasa's life, for all the rest took place in a realm beyond pictures and stories. He never again left the forest" (612).[1] Dasa has reached the point where his life leaves behind that mode of being which can be chronicled narratively. The lived peace, the certainty beyond friction and change, the wholeness of wisdom—these cannot be conveyed in plot or palpable image. This perception, with which Hesse's novel closes, focuses for us the central thematic concerns within *The Glass Bead Game*: the nature of the story and of the hero, and above all, the

---

[1] References throughout are to Hesse, *Das Glasperlenspiel* (Frankfurt: Suhrkamp Taschenbuch, 1973). My translations are heavily indebted to the version by Richard and Clara Winston, *The Glass Bead Game* (Harmondsworth, 1972).

relationship of that life, of that selfhood, to notions of human and cultural wholeness.

The story is told by a narrator who belongs to the elite province of Castalia and who writes this account some time after the death of the great Magister Ludi. The opening few pages of the novel are devoted to the problem of Knecht's significance within Castalia. We learn that "obliteration of individuality, the maximum integration of the individual into the hierarchy of the educators and scholars, has ever been one of the guiding principles of our spiritual life " (8). The narrator is at pains to distinguish his biographical enterprise from that of earlier writers:

> Certainly, what nowadays we understand by personality is something significantly different from what the biographers and historians of earlier times meant by it. For them and especially for the writers of those days who had a distinct taste for biography, the essence of a personality seems to have been deviance, abnormality, uniqueness, in fact all too often the pathological. We moderns, on the other hand, do not even speak of major personalities until we encounter men who have gone beyond all original and idiosyncratic qualities to achieve the greatest possible integration into the generality, the greatest possible service to the suprapersonal. (9)

This is, I would suggest, a passage that reminds us very much of the passionate onslaught on individuation that informs Stifter's *Indian Summer*. Hesse's narrator, while he at times pays lip service to the notion of personality, essentially writes from a position in which the manifestations of individuality are to be regretted as some kind of pre-Castalian aberration. It follows from this (and from comments he makes on bourgeois degeneration in the "newspaper supplement age") that our narrator is bitterly critical of the bourgeois convention of storytelling because it implies a cult of *individual* selfhood. The narrator asserts that he is interested in Knecht insofar as he is the paradigm of the suprapersonal life of Castalia. And yet, of course, Knecht's life is the story not only of "impersonal" service to Castalia, but of defection precisely in the name of *personal* commitment and responsibility. The narrator's account enacts a largely unacknowledged paradox: Knecht's life is, in spite of, or, more accurately, because of Castalia, a "life" in the old bourgeois sense. Which is another way of saying that *The Glass Bead Game* opens as a work written against the demands of traditional novel expectation, but progresses to the point of validating the novel genre as personal biography.

This tension takes us very much to the heart of the theme and narrative technique of Hesse's novel. It has been suggested, most notably by Theodore Ziolkowski in what is by far the liveliest and most suggestive account of Hesse's art,[2] that the discrepancy between avowed narrative intention and actual narrative realization is to be explained in terms of the prolonged gestation and growth process of the book. This is, of course, a possible explanation; but I find it deeply unsatisfying. Writers are, after all, capable of rewriting earlier sections of a work if this is demanded by a later change in overall conception. In my view, the narrative tension of *The Glass Bead Game* was not obliterated for significant artistic reasons (which are, incidentally, particularly suggestive for any understanding of the Bildungsroman tradition). The closing stages of Knecht's life, unlike those of

[2] Ziolkowski, *The Novels of Hermann Hesse: A Study in Theme and Structure* (Princeton, 1965), 294. Ziolkowski's argument has been challenged (see G. W. Field, "On the Genesis of *Das Glasperlenspiel*," *German Quarterly*, 41 [1968], 673-88). Whether Ziolkowski is right or wrong about the genesis of the novel, he is, in my view, *interpretatively* right to stress the tension at work in the book; other critics have somehow dissolved that tension into serene thematic progression.

Prince Dasa's, take place within the realm of stories and pictures. However much the conclusion may be symbolic of Knecht's "service" in its truest and finest sense, yet it also reports an *event* that is both irrevocable and concrete.[3]

The Glass Bead Game opens with a leisurely statement of Castalian beliefs. The narrator proudly proclaims himself a Castalian, a "modern," that is, someone who inhabits a world that has gone beyond the bourgeois fetish of individuality. (Thereby, of course, he implicitly recognizes the historical *donnée* of his own intellectual position, and, as we shall see, history emerges as one of the major themes of the novel.) The highest expression of Castalia is to be found in the Glass Bead Game which is so much its intellectual and spiritual center. We are told that the game had its precursors wherever and whenever scholars and intellectuals looked beyond the confines of their specific, specialist disciplines in order to find some integral principle that binds together human culture into a total, synchronic phenomenon. We learn that "the symbols and formulas of the Glass Bead Game combined structurally, musically, and philosophically within the framework of a universal language, were nourished by all the sciences and arts, and sought in play to achieve perfection, pure being, the fullness of reality" (40-41). The game is the expression

---

[3] See Mark Boulby's contention that the ending of the novel involves "service . . . of the self" (*Hermann Hesse: His Mind and Art* [Ithaca and London, 1967], 320). Many critics have commented on Knecht's break with Castalia. It has been variously suggested that the ending is to be seen as a higher and truer fulfillment of Knecht's mission of pedagogic service, that it represents a commitment to life and practical activity, or that it negates the spiritual significance of Castalia, thereby relativizing the whole import of the novel. All these arguments have pertinence, but to me they are slightly off center. The real force of Knecht's decision can, I think, only be sensed in terms of the kind of cultural debate with novel tradition which I have stressed in my analysis. Within this framework, the narrator's Castalian ideology brings into focus the whole spectrum of issues suggested by Knecht's act of defection.

of the Castalian "tendency toward universality" (88): people of intellectual potential are encouraged to devote themselves to free study of even the most abstruse topics because their work, however esoteric, does feed into the generality of the scholarly community. (We are reminded here in some ways of the Society of the Tower in *Wilhelm Meister*: the context of the community provides the wholeness by being the intersection of many discrete lives and interests.)

To this Glass Bead Game Josef Knecht offers devoted and strenuous service, although he is not unmindful of the dangers in the Castalian way of life. These dangers are manifold, and they become the psychological substance of Knecht's unease, which will finally produce the break with Castalia. Knecht comes to see that any attempt at realizing a totality within the life of man must, by definition, operate with abstractions from discrete, individual experience. Abstraction, bloodlessness, and ahistoricity are therefore the besetting sins of Castalia. (One thinks of the present-day battles of Structuralists and Marxists, in which the role of history likewise becomes more often than not the essential bone of contention.) Many of Knecht's reservations are stated in discursive form in his open letter to the authorities of Castalia. But these vital thematic concerns are also underpinned in a variety of ways. History itself becomes a source of constant pedagogic debate in the novel. From Pater Jacobus, Knecht "learned to see the present and his own life as historical realities" (178). The process of this specific learning is not an easy one for Knecht. Jacobus at one point sternly reproaches him: "You treat world history as a mathematician does mathematics, in which nothing but laws and formulas exist, no reality, no good and evil, no time, no yesterday, no tomorrow, nothing but an eternal flat, mathematical present" (179). Knecht comes to realize that Castalia is part of history, that it is *of necessity* a historical phenomenon: "we forget

that we ourselves are a part of history, that we are the
product of growth and we are condemned to perish if
we lose the capacity for growth and change" (386). He
will live out that principle of growth and change by his
act of defection.

The deepest import of the theme of history, however,
takes us into the very heart of the narrative tension
which informs *The Glass Bead Game*. When Knecht discovers history as an ontological dimension, he discovers
something that not only modifies the intellectual teaching of Castalia but also radically transforms his own understanding of himself. Knecht's perception of history
as a general principle entails the vital notion of personal
historicity. Knecht acknowledges that he himself has a
"history," a story, a linear chronology of experiences for
which he is responsible. His defection from Castalia not
only expresses his intellectual disagreement with the
province but also enacts the personal, existential con-
comitant of his convictions: he asserts that he has an individuality, a story which cannot be obliterated in the
pictureless and storyless world of Castalian ideals.

Early in the novel, the narrator declares that "the writing of history—however soberly it is done and however
sincere the desire for objectivity—remains literature.
History's third dimension is always fiction" (45-46).
One is here reminded of Kant's "cosmopolitan history"
which threatens to become a novel! Moreover, we could
turn the narrator's statement around to say that all literature, and for our purposes this applies particularly to
narrative literature, must partake of history, must in
other words be concerned with the historicity of a life,
with its chronology, with its lived sequence. Knecht,
despite the narrator's opening polemics, is the hero of a
novel. However much his life may be directed toward
the service of suprapersonal goals and ideas, he has a
personal story which the narrator chronicles, thereby
giving thematic enactment to the values inherent in

Knecht's life: the protagonist becomes the supreme Magister Ludi, but only to repudiate his eminence and the principles which he has hitherto served.

Knecht is helped to overcome an early crisis in his life by talking with the Music Master. The latter reveals something of his past and of his personal difficulties and uncertainties. What comforts Knecht is the realization "that even a demigod, even a Master, had once been young, and capable of erring" (109). That personal history which antedates the Music Master's translation into Castalian greatness is made up of conflict and uncertainty and groping for insight. The story has the friction of struggle and conflict, of erring, and it therefore antedates the attained goal in which the self is submerged in the universal principle that is Castalia. Knecht's story is interesting precisely for those aspects which do not easily fit in with the Castalian ideology which the narrator so stridently affirmed at the beginning of the novel.

We sense the full measure of Knecht's difficulty with Castalia in his various dealings with the authorities shortly before his resignation. Master Alexander attacks Knecht: "You have an excessive sense of your own person, a dependence on it" (438). The conflict between Alexander and Knecht is irreparable because it is one of fundamental principle. The President also reproaches Knecht: "Here you are speaking about your own life, and you mention scarcely anything but private, subjective experiences, personal wishes, personal developments and decisions. I really had no idea that a Castalian of your rank could see himself and his life in such a light" (440). Knecht answers by invoking precisely those principles which are anathema to the President: "I am trying to show you the path I have trodden as an individual, which has led me out of Waldzell and will lead me out of Castalia tomorrow" (440). Knecht asserts both the reality and the value of the individual path in answer to the uncomprehending Castalian ideology. Some

of this ideology remains with our narrator, particularly
in his somewhat defensive opening statements. It is, of
course, one of the deepest ironies of the book that the
narrator, in spite of himself, chronicles the life of a man
whose intractable individuality and historical self-
assertion transcends Castalian ideology and is potentially the source of the province's regeneration. Yet one
wonders whether Castalia would be able to absorb the
import of Knecht's life. The narrator's empathy with his
protagonist may on occasion take him beyond the confines of that somewhat defensive Castalian position
which he espoused at the opening. But on the other
hand, the ending to Knecht's life can somehow be de-
prived of its sting by being incorporated into a manageable legend. The title of the book gives continued primacy to the cultural institution—the Glass Bead
Game—while relegating Knecht's life to the subtitle,
"Attempt at a Biography of the Magister Ludi Josef
Knecht together with Knecht's posthumous papers,
edited by Hermann Hesse." Certainly, the opening
pages give no hint that the significance of Knecht's experience has been seized. Thereby a narrative tension is
established which heightens the significance of those
moments when the narrator glimpses the complexity
and resonance of Knecht's life.[4] At one point, for example, he praises Knecht:

> Knecht was a great, an exemplary administrator, an
> honor to his high office, an irreproachable Glass
> Bead Game Master. But he saw and felt the glory of
> Castalia, even as he devoted himself to it, as an im-
> periled greatness that was on the wane. He did
> not participate in its life thoughtlessly and unknow-

---

[4] See Hans Mayer, "Hesse's *Glasperlenspiel* oder die Wiederbegeg-
nung," in *Ansichten: Zur Literatur der Zeit* (Reinbek bei Hamburg,
1962), esp. 52. Throughout my analysis I am indebted to Mayer's essay, which suggests the full range of immanent contradictions in the
novel.

ingly, as did the great majority of his fellow Casta-
lians, for he knew about its origins and history, was
conscious of it as a historical entity, subject to time,
washed and eroded by time's remorseless power.
This sensitivity to the living experience of historical
processes and this feeling for his own self and activity as a cell carried along and working with the
stream of growth and transformation had ripened
within him and become conscious in the course of
his historical studies and under the influence of the
great Pater Jacobus. The predisposition to such
consciousness, its germs had been present within
him long before. Whoever genuinely tries to explore the meaning of that life, its idiosyncrasy, will
easily discover these germs. (288-89)

Such observations on the part of the narrator are, as it
were, generated by the story he has to tell; they remain
glimpses which are not allowed to ripen into a fully articulated attitude. They are moments which bring into
focus the narrative tension of the book, and that tension
is thematic enrichment rather than artistic inconsistency
on Hesse's part. Over and over again we sense that the
narrator is impelled to recognize qualities which conflict
with the Castalian ideal. One example is the narrator's
remark about Plinio Designori at the beginning of Chapter 10: "nevertheless, he was not simply a failure. In de-
feat and renunciation he had, in spite of everything, acquired a specific profile, a particular destiny" (350). For
the narrator of the opening pages, "a specific profile, a
particular destiny" could hardly have constituted any
kind of achievement. Or again, toward the end of the
novel, the narrator comments on the void left in Castalia
by Knecht's withdrawal:

The laconic, sensible remarks [of Knecht's final tes-
tament to the province] stood there in neat, small
letters, the words and handwriting just as uniquely

and unmistakably typical of Joseph Knecht as his
face, his voice, his gait. The Board would scarcely
find a man of his stature for his successor; real masters and real personalities were all too rare, and
each one was a matter of good luck and a pure gift,
even here in Castalia, the province of the elite. (448)

The remarks sound valedictory: the emphasis falls on
precisely those details that are unique to Knecht, and
the closing sentence implicitly links "real masters" and
"real personalities." The narrator, while only rarely
acknowledging as much, has moved a long way from
his opening remarks on the questionableness of personality. The story told in this novel is of growth, movement, change. And the narrative voice becomes an ac-
companiment to those processes; it grows and changes
with the life it is obliged to chronicle.

Once a year each student in Castalia has to write a fictional "life" in which he explores certain potentialities
he feels to be inherent in himself. Our narrator notes
that "while writing these lives many an author took his
first steps into the land of self-knowledge" (120). We are
allowed direct access to three such lives, all of them by
Knecht. It is tempting to assume that these lives are an
unequivocal celebration of a certain goal, of the decisive
attainment of self-knowledge on the part of the protagonist. In this way the stories can be invested with a
straightforwardly didactic import. Yet one might view
their significance differently and stress that the essential
interest in the lives is the way rather than the goal, for
the simple reason that the attained goal implies an integrity of being and purpose, an absence of friction and
wandering that is foreign to the specifically *narrative* act.
Certainly, the story of Josef Knecht is important precisely because it is a *story*. The pattern in this life is, I
would suggest, one familiar to us: Wilhelm Meister
emerges from the Society of the Tower feeling as in-

tractably unenlightened and baffled as ever; Hans Castorp gradually forgets the snow vision; Josef Knecht, with full moral and intellectual knowledge of what he is doing, repudiates that special province which is devoted to spiritual wholeness and harmony. The friction between story and totality, between *Nacheinander* and *Nebeneinander*, between, in the terms of Hesse's novel, historicity and the Castalian ideal, has profound implications for both plot and characterization in the novel. And these implications are, as I have tried to suggest, structurally central to the German Bildungsroman.

Virtually all of Hesse's novels are concerned with human striving for integrity and wholeness. In this sense his fictional world can be profitably viewed within the context of the Bildungsroman tradition. A novel such as *The Steppenwolf* would, I think, interlock suggestively with a number of the issues I have been raising. (It would, for example, be interesting to compare the function of the theater in this novel and in *Wilhelm Meister's Apprenticeship*: in both, I suspect, the theater has special thematic significance within the hero's quest for perspective on his own selfhood. One wonders also about the role of the "Immortals" as emissaries from a world that knows of the complex coexistence of specific talents and proclivities. In this sense they are akin to the Society of the Tower. Indeed, both have in common a certain sententiousness, in the maxims to which Wilhelm is referred, and in the "Treatise" which Harry Haller acquires.) But I have chosen to restrict my discussion of Hesse to *The Glass Bead Game* for one very simple reason. To me, it is the one novel of Hesse's in which the Bildungsroman tradition occupies a specific and overtly indicated place in the novel fiction. The name of its hero, Knecht (servant) is a quizzical echo of that of Goethe's hero, Meister (master), and Knecht becomes Master of the Bead Game. Moreover, the Castalian province clearly recalls the "Pedagogic Province" of *Wilhelm Meister's Travels*. The stress throughout *The Glass Bead Game* on learning and growth clearly announces an indebtedness to the Bildungsroman. When Josef Knecht becomes involved with Plinio Designori, we read that he has "come to feel that this other boy would mean something important to him, perhaps something fine, an enlargement of his horizon, insight or illumination, perhaps also temptation and danger" (98). Here we sense the characteristic principle that informs so much of the hero's experience in the Bildungsroman: the other figure is important for the protagonist's growth and self-understanding, he matters insofar as he catalyzes a certain inner potential slumbering within the hero. Even the eccentric Tegularius is important in this way for Knecht: he is "a small open window that looked out upon new vistas" (295). One wonders also whether there are not specific echoes in Hesse's text. When Knecht reflects on the primitive world outside the confines of Castalia we read: "this primitive world was innate in every man; everyone felt something of it in his own heart, had some curiosity about it, some nostalgia for it, some sympathy with it. The true task was to be fair to it, to keep a place for it in one's heart, but still not relapse into it" (104). Both the ideas here, and their formulation, call to mind Hans Castorp's insights in the "Snow" chapter of *The Magic Mountain*. (Moreover, Thomas Mann himself figures as a distinguished Castalian under the thinly veiled pseudonym of Thomas Van der Trave.) Finally, when Plinio asks Knecht, "which of us is really the authentic and valid human being, you or me? Every so often I doubt that either of us is" (340), he raises one of the paramount intellectual issues of the Bildungsroman tradition.

Moreover, one should note that the concern in Hesse's novel for *Geist* marks it as a work unmistakably embedded in the generality of the German intellectual tradition. *Geist* is a realm which allows the limiting dimension of the real to be transcended by the abundant potentiality of human consciousness. Even Plinio expresses his lasting indebtedness to Castalia "for not letting anything coerce me into a course of studies designed to prepare the student as thoroughly as possible in the shortest possible time for a speciality in which he could earn his livelihood, and to stamp out whatever sense of freedom and universality he may have had" (325). Castalia is, then, a realm which allows for "freedom and universality" in answer to the constrictions of everyday social practicalities. But at the same time, it is a world dangerously determined to insulate itself from actualities; it is an ivory tower, an elite province which will not acknowledge its own embeddedness in history as the given dimension of human being and activity. In this novel Hesse offers an affectionate, yet deeply critical, examination of a familiar pattern in German thinking. The all-pervasive presence of the Bildungsroman is the measure of the specificity of Hesse's engagement with the German tradition. The tensions that inform the novel suggest precisely his uncertainties and misgivings. And these are also the tensions present in the major Bildungsromane. In its finest examples, this novel tradition is never an unproblematic odyssey toward human wholeness. None of the major novels ever unquestioningly endorses that strident equation, made by Fritz Tegularius, of "real history" with the "timeless history of the mind" (303). Knecht has *his* "history"—as do Agathon, Wilhelm Meister, and the other protagonists. The *Nacheinander* of plot, of personal history, is simply not an eradicable quantity.

One final comment about the theme of history in *The Glass Bead Game*: the novel is, of course, set at some future date when the dilemmas of bourgeois individualism (as outlined in the narrator's denunciation of the

decline into the "newspaper supplement age") have
been transcended in the creation of Castalia, the ideal
province.[5] Hesse takes as the prehistory of Castalia precisely those bourgeois-individualist values which produced in the Bildungsroman the attempt to mediate between individual and totality, between the increasing
specialization and restriction of practical life and the
need for human wholeness and community. By project-
ing that future world of Castalia, Hesse postulates,
as it were, the actual attainment of the so frequently
intimated (but hardly ever realized) teleology of the
great Bildungsromane. Yet, precisely because of its
provenance, Castalia remains a problematic utopia, one
whose ideals are but the wish-dream of that bourgeois
culture from which it has sprung. In every sense, then,
Castalia has a history: paradoxically, its very aversion to
history serves to reveal its roots in history. In this context, Knecht's life takes on a truly exemplary function.
He is offered the opportunity of lasting escape from the
world of practical reality by being absorbed into an elite
enclave dedicated to spiritual harmony and totality. But
he comes to repudiate that opportunity as a falsity. In
The Glass Bead Game the aspirations of the Bildungsroman, and their inherent questionableness, find intense,
thoroughgoing exploration. And once again, the result
is a work shot through with an unremitting narrative
argument with, against, and ultimately for the novel
form with its bedrock credo of the story told in chronological, that is, historical, sequence. The theme of history in *The Glass Bead Game* is, then, intimately bound
up with its own historicity as a literary text. For like

[5] Field, "On the Genesis of *Das Glasperlenspiel*," has shown how
Hesse, in the gradual reworking of his material, removed the specific
references to the 1930s, to nationalism, political brutality, and Nazism.
In place of historical specificity we are given a cultural-typological
analysis which, in my view, suggests the generality of cultural values
from which the Bildungsroman derives. The reworking process is a
further illustration of that urgent debate with novel tradition which is
so central to *Das Glasperlenspiel*.

Thomas Mann's *Doktor Faustus* (1947), this novel, first published in 1943, is Hesse's urgently critical examination of his own intellectual roots. It was an examination necessitated by the course of European, and particularly German, history. In both novels (and the same can be said of Mann's specific exploration of the Bildungsroman tradition in *The Magic Mountain*), present understanding involved activation of and debate with the German tradition.

Hesse's *The Glass Bead Game* is in this way very much a part of the heart-searching and self-examination that followed the collapse of the Third Reich. One urgent feature of this debate was the question of whether there were, so to speak, two Germanies, a "good" and a "bad," or whether there was but one Germany, the evil self being inextricably intertwined with the good. In this context one can appreciate the special force and cogency of Hesse's taking issue with the Bildungsroman tradition. This novel genre was surely one paradigm for an exploration of the "German problem": in one sense it was the repository of the great humanistic tradition of Germany, providing a link with the eighteenth-century *Humanitätsideal*; but in another sense it was the embodiment of that questionable inwardness, of that lack of thoroughgoing concern with practical affairs and political facts which had so bedeviled the German nation.

The resonance of Hesse's undertaking can be measured by recalling the closing pages of Friedrich Meinecke's *The Great Catastrophe* (1946), in which Meinecke looks for a way forward and out of the devastation that has befallen Germany. The emphasis of his solution is characteristic: "Everything, yes everything, depends upon an intensified development of our inner existence."[6] He suggests the need for Germany to draw new strength from its Golden Age of Weimar:

---

[6] Meinecke, *The Great Catastrophe*, trans. Sidney Fay (Boston, 1963), 115.

The heights of the Goethe period and of the highly gifted generation living in it were reached by many individual men, bound together merely in small circles by ties of friendship. They strove for and to a large degree realized the ideal of a personal and wholly individual culture. This culture was thought of as having at the same time a universal human meaning and content.[7]

Meinecke goes on to speak of the need for organizations to promote this renewal of German spiritual identity. But the relationship to "organization" is characteristically grudging. What is essentially involved is German *Bildung* in all its inwardness: "does organization alone promote spiritual culture? Does not spiritual culture demand a sphere for individual inclination, for solitude, and for the deepening of one's self?"[8] Insofar as Meinecke explores the practical question of how to restore the integrity of the nation, he suggests the setting up of "Goethe communities," which could meet "at a late Sunday afternoon hour, and if at all possible in a church,"[9] in order to listen to German music and poetry being performed and read. Beyond this he does not go: "I shall not sketch this further here, in order not to anticipate the free creative activity of individuals. The whole idea must start with individuals, personalities, the special few who first build among themselves only one such Goethe community, and then let it develop here in one form, there in another."[10] Meinecke offers here an unreflective reinstatement of the ideal of *Bildung*: social and political life is to find its center of gravity in an elite group of spiritual leaders bound together by a special distinction and wholeness.

Where Meinecke can take up a tradition which, for him, is still left intact, Hesse finds himself obliged to

[7] Ibid., 115.   [8] Ibid., 116.
[9] Ibid., 120.   [10] Ibid., 121.

mount a critique of that very tradition from within. As I hope my inquiry has suggested, the authors of the major Bildungsromane were often more differentiated and questioning in their espousal of *Bildung* than were the theoreticians, the philosophers, or, as in Meinecke's case, the historians.

══ VIII ══
Conclusion

The German Bildungsroman represents a remarkable and very special achievement within the overall context of European novel writing after 1770. To English-speaking readers it is, as I have already suggested, a somewhat alien phenomenon, the perfect example of German "depth" and learnedness. It is a novel fiction that seems to lack notably that "vital capacity for experience, [that] reverent openness before life, [that] marked moral intensity" which for F. R. Leavis is so characteristic of the English novel at its best.[1] It is therefore hardly surprising that when English critics have voiced specific reservations about German culture, their criticisms have focused principally on the cult of *Bildung* and on the Bildungsroman as its essential fictional expression. Goethe is the most frequently selected target. Walter Bagehot said of him in 1850: "He moved hither and hither through life, but he was always a man apart. . . . In every scene he was there, and he made it clear that he was there, with a reserve, and as a stranger. He went there to *experience*."[2] This criticism is expressed with even greater polemical fervor by D. H. Lawrence when he speaks of Goethe's "boundless ego" and attacks *Wilhelm Meister* for "the utter incapacity for any development of contact with any other human being, which is particularly bourgeois and Goethean."[3] One should note that the English are not alone in their skepticism about the German Bildungsroman. It is fitting that Thomas Mann, as someone deeply embedded in that

---

[1] Leavis, *The Great Tradition* (Harmondsworth, 1962), 17.
[2] Quoted in W. H. Bruford, *The German Tradition of Self-Cultivation* (Cambridge, 1975), 42.
[3] Ibid., 42.

tradition, should voice criticism of the genre: "It is well known that you [Germans] live for the sake of experience—and not for the sake of life. Self-enrichment is what you are out for. C'est ça, you do not seem to realize that that is really egoism, and that one day you will be revealed as enemies of humanity."[4] The speaker here is not Thomas Mann *in propria persona*: the words are spoken by Frau Chauchat to Hans Castorp, the "mediocre" hero of the most complex and elusive of all Bildungsromane. From within the fictional employment of the genre, Mann's criticisms accord with the objections of "outsiders."

I want to suggest, however, that precisely because of its foreignness the Bildungsroman is a novel tradition which can have special, almost provocative, importance for the reader who comes to it from the outside. Indeed, I have found that the German Bildungsroman can speak with immediacy to present-day university students. The elusiveness of the learning and growing process, the alternation of insight with a sense of confusion and inconsequentiality, the vexed question of the relationship between knowing and doing, between the pedagogic community and the generality of the social experience outside its walls—these are thematic issues which strike a chord in the minds of present-day students. Their responsiveness is symptomatic of a number of more general factors which make the Bildungsroman tradition accessible to us. First, I think it important to stress that the discursiveness, the intellectual debate which is so much a feature of the Bildungsroman has by now become acceptable, even commonplace, within the novel form. Many twentieth-century novels operate with a kind of "essayism" which allows us to see the Bildungsroman not as a German aberration but as a tradition which anticipates modern developments. Indeed, two more re-

[4] *Der Zauberberg*, II (Berlin, 1924), 425.

cent studies of the novel suggest that such self-reflective discursiveness has long been a feature of the novel tradition as a whole.[5] Second, it seems to me that the Bildungsroman anticipates certain thematic developments within contemporary fiction. It is a novel form superbly equipped to handle the flux of character, as opposed to manageable development. It can render the curious indeterminacy of the growing process, the unexpectedly integrative force of random experience which intimates—yet never quite confers—the sense of the self as a coherent and intact entity. I shall return to this "modern" feel of the Bildungsroman in the excursus which closes this book. Finally, it must be stressed that the German Bildungsroman is one of the cardinal documents of bourgeois literacy. It is a novel genre which embodies some of the deepest aspirations of bourgeois society. For this reason it tells us a great deal about Germany from 1770 on, and, by implication, it raises a number of issues which are very much with us today as the strains and stresses of our society become ever more apparent. It is to this latter aspect of the Bildungsroman tradition that I wish to turn in these concluding remarks.

Albert Ward, in his study *Book Production, Fiction and the German Reading Public 1740-1800,*[6] has provided us with an admirable picture of the social and economic circumstances of the book trade around the time when the Bildungsroman came to prominence. He stresses that the German novel of the seventeenth century was essentially written by and for aristocrats and scholars. The early decades of the eighteenth century show the dominance in German book production of scholarly

---

[5] Gerhart von Graevenitz, *Die Setzung des Subjekts: Untersuchungen zur Romantheorie* (Tübingen, 1973); Robert Alter, *Partial Magic: The Novel as a Self-Conscious Genre* (Berkeley and London, 1975).

[6] (Oxford, 1974).

and, especially, religious works. The novel was at that time felt to be profane, degrading entertainment; it was "mere" story. Gradually, however, a number of decisive changes in sensibility and taste began to make themselves felt. In the first half of the eighteenth century a general process of secularization occurred as the hold of formal religion over the middle-class imagination began to slacken. One factor in this process was pietism and the importance it attached to the inner life, to individual capacity for feeling. An important consequence was a growing popular taste for diaries and letter writing. This predilection was in turn reflected in fictional forms where biographical and epistolary conventions dominated. The opening decades of the eighteenth century also saw the growth of moral weeklies and of journalism. This was, as Ward suggests,[7] symptomatic of the transition from an age of patronage to the more open marketplace in which the publisher was the patron. Daniel Defoe's *Robinson Crusoe* (1719) was one of the signal successes within this new climate: it is both a splendid adventure story, with a strong exotic appeal, and also a narrative of a soul's search for God. Here, then, we find a secular work of real interest which had the moral and spiritual seriousness to make it acceptable to the solid citizen.

In one sense, the growth of the novel form to popularity in eighteenth-century Germany is the story of the gradual self-liberation of the German *Bürger* from the constraints of religion—to the point where his life, both in its social and psychological aspects, became a worthy subject for literary exploration. This loosening of the authority of the church was further underpinned by the *Aufklärung* (Enlightenment) which became an intellectual force in the second half of the eighteenth century and fostered a critical attitude toward tradition and dogma. Independent thought was encouraged. More-

[7] Ibid., 28.

over, when Christianity was invoked, it was as the guarantor of man's ethical principles, not as a metaphysical system. Morals and dispassionate good sense became decisive arbiters in human affairs. Such factors were, of course, part of an important change in European sensibility as a whole.[8] But one should also note that there are a number of factors specific to the German context. Ward makes the point that the broader German public, unlike the English, showed little interest in good literature, that the major works of German idealism and classicism appealed only to the educated elite of the middle classes—teachers, doctors, clergymen, civil servants.[9] Popular taste was catered to by the veritable torrent of trivial literature that appeared in the last thirty years or so of the eighteenth century. It is important to remember this because it suggests that the aesthetic and intellectual revolution generated by bourgeois-liberal thinking (the breeding ground of the European novel) was nowhere near as extensive or broadly based in Germany as in England. Hence, novelists such as Wieland or theoreticians such as Blanckenburg were aware of having to invest immense aesthetic labor in order to redeem the prosaic and debased form of the novel. Moreover, because of the relative half-heartedness of the bourgeois liberation in Germany, the great achievements of German bourgeois literature, such as *Agathon* or *Wilhelm Meister's Apprenticeship*, have much more obviously a "learned" and intellectual flavor than do the novels of, say, Defoe, Fielding, or Smollett. The classical ideal in German literature was a good deal more rarefied, more divorced from the immediate texture of social experience than were its English counterparts. Indeed, *Bildung*, that key concept of German

[8] The English situation has, for instance, been admirably documented by Ian Watt in his *The Rise of the Novel* (Harmondsworth, 1963).

[9] Ward, *Book Production*, 133.

bourgeois thinking, involved a belief in inwardness as the source of human distinction. In this sense, it retained a quasi-religious flavor which did much to reduce its social and, above all, political resonance.

Clearly, it is not enough simply to condemn Germany for failing to develop the kind of enterprisingly enlightened thinking of the English middle classes. One has to note the very considerable differences between the two societies. Two more recent studies help us to perceive the key factors. Heinrich Heffter, in his detailed study of German notions of self-government, makes the point that nineteenth-century Germany was dominated by an all-pervasive and authoritarian bureaucracy and that even the Prussian liberal reforms of the last three decades of the century were shaped by the bureaucracy to the extent that reform became, paradoxically, "a hindrance to the fulfillment of liberal strivings."[10] Heffter summarizes those essential characteristics of nineteenth-century German society which distinguished it from the rest of Europe:

> The backwardness of constitutional development in Germany compared with Western Europe was linked above all with the incomplete emergence of the middle class. The bourgeoisie, here too the essential vehicle of the liberal movement, lived in a narrow, cosy, "Biedermeier" world in which only the first stirrings of the industrial revolution were making themselves felt. The dominant stratum of the bourgeoisie was the professional men and the dignitaries of the upper middle classes who stood for the values of developed and abundant culture [Bildung] rather than for strong economically defined class interests. [Friedrich] Dahlmann, the most important North German spokesman for

[10] Heffter, *Die deutsche Selbstverwaltung im 19. Jahrhundert* (Stuttgart, 1950), 643.

pre-March liberalism, gave characteristic expression to the aspiring consciousness of this ʻmiddle class when he praised it as the "center of the people," as the "center of gravity of the state." According to him, the middle class had "united within its armory a knowledge of traditional spiritual values with the fortune of the old aristocracy." Should it, however, seek "to assert itself as a mass movement," it would transform itself into "a mob devoid of both culture and fortune." . . . A bourgeoisie according to the model of Western Europe—as the dominant class within a developed industrial and capitalist economy—was only growing very slowly.[11]

The features which Heffter mentions here are almost universally invoked in any account of the *deutsche Misere*. And it is important to note that *Bildung* is seen as a cornerstone of that quiescent, unpolitical bourgeois ideology which made German liberalism such a half-hearted phenomenon.

Mack Walker, in his cogent study *German Home Towns*,[12] gives a thorough and perceptive account of the social and political conditions which account for the lack of an energetic, enlightened bourgeoisie in Germany. He insists that nineteenth-century Germany (with the exception of Prussia and Bavaria) was very much the "individualized land" of Riehl's social geography.[13] It was, in other words, a society sustained by the characteristic infrastructure of the Holy Roman Empire, the small, organic community hostile to modern law and administration, to modern population movement and growth. As, inevitably, the demographic changes associated with industrialization began to make themselves felt, the small town ethos reacted with a radi-

---

[11] Ibid., 168.   [12] (Ithaca and London), 1971.
[13] Ibid., 1. The particularism of Germany means that the nation existed in the cultural and linguistic (but not political) sense.

calized particularism. In this reaction, Walker argues, one feels the spirit of the Holy Roman Empire at work, that of "resistance by diversity to power and change in Germany."[14] One has, in other words, a situation in which absolutism coexisted with particularism, even eccentricity. Or, more accurately, one should perhaps say that the whole (the state) willed the individual selfhood of its component parts, while the component parts found their validation in the presence of the state as guarantor of their particularism. This characteristic relationship is one that finds fictional reworking and exploration in the Bildungsroman as a novel genre which evokes a world rarely alien to the protagonist's quest for an organic unfolding of his individual selfhood. At one point Walker invokes the all-important concept of the whole man as characteristic of the "home town ethos": "Hometownsmen did not have the multiple standards and compartmentalized lives that so many modern moral and social critics deplore: one set of standards for church on Sunday, another for relations and friends, another for business relations. They were whole men, integrated personalities, caught like so many flies in a three-dimensional web of community."[15] This comment, I think, brings us close to the heart of the fictional undertaking of the Bildungsroman. One is reminded, for example, of the contention of countless critics that the Bildungsroman is the critical voice of specifically German humanism, desperately protesting against the damaging inroads made by modern industrial society into human wholeness and integration. Walker's conclusion is pertinent here: "the ubiquitous yearning for organic wholeness seems the most important legacy of hometown history to twentieth-century Germany."[16]

Both Heffter and Walker have concerned themselves with specific features of German society which account for the generation of certain moral and intellectual at-

[14] Ibid., 16.   [15] Ibid., 106.
[16] Ibid., 426.

titudes. A number of other analyses explore the ideas and concepts themselves. Hajo Holborn, in his essay "Der deutsche Idealismus in sozialgeschichtlicher Beleuchtung,"[17] is at pains to stress a number of features of the *intellectual* landscape of Germany that distinguish it from the rest of Europe. He argues, for example, that those who raised their voices in late eighteenth-century Germany were only a small segment of the middle class; it was the intellectuals—professors, teachers, clergymen—who made themselves heard. Characteristically, they pleaded for *intellectual*, not political, freedoms. These were, so to speak, bureaucratically protected voices, who were careful to demand only such freedoms as partake of the inner, spiritual life of the individual. Moreover, Holborn insists, the German *Aufklärung* had a closer relationship to religion than did its European counterparts. In its respect for religion, German idealism became "a passionate struggle for a new religious interpretation of life."[18] Even liberal theology was sustained by "the same culturally-aristocratic atmosphere."[19] There was no equivalent to, say, the social engagement of Wesley's Methodists in England. Holborn concludes that Christian socialism did not develop in Germany and that Marx sought to establish a philosophical, rather than religious, legitimation of that process by which the working classes achieve dignity and self-realization. Indeed, over and over again one is forced to recognize that a gulf separated the intellectual revolution of German idealism from any kind of concern with society or politics. The intellectual questioning coalesces to form that "above all intellectually and aesthetically inclined idealism with its individualistic culture of inwardness."[20] The bourgeois, then, became

---

[17] *Historische Zeitschrift*, 174 (1952), 359ff.

[18] Ibid., 370. And hence, *Bildung* became a secular version of the quest for spiritual salvation.

[19] Ibid., 371.   [20] Ibid., 380.

representative by his very inwardness, and that inwardness responded to what one critic has called "an initially almost exclusively academic literary Enlightenment which characteristically conferred status and prestige."[21]

The foregoing arguments help to account for the curiously fastidious dislike of politics, the equation of seriousness and value with inwardness, that is so characteristic of German bourgeois culture. *Geist* is an inward realm, a vantage point from which the narrowness and insufficiency of the practical world can be transcended. Yet this is not the whole story. Indeed, there is a fascinating oscillation in the German worship of *Geist*. On the one hand, it can be the cipher for the withdrawal from any engagement with the real world, but on the other, it can be the agency which legitimates the social world by absolutizing it. It is a curiously "all or nothing" relationship. The affirmative possibility, the almost metaphysical transfiguration of the state into a spiritual entity, is documented by Leonard Krieger in his brilliant study, *The German Idea of Freedom*.[22] He insists that *Libertät* was the key concept of the principalities within the Holy Roman Empire, one which made "the idea of liberty not the polar antithesis but the historical associate of princely authority."[23] From this followed the ominous pairing of "secular submission and spiritual independence."[24] Krieger identifies as a characteristic tendency in German thought the readiness to extend "the power of the state in direct proportion with the increasing recognition of individual rights: the greater the individual's rights, the larger his responsibility, and the larger therefore the role of the state as the guarantor of

---

[21] Gerhart von Graevenitz, "Interlichkeit und Öffentlichkeit: Aspekte deutscher bürgerlicher Literatur im frühen 18. Jahrhundert," *DVLG*, 49 (1975), 81*.

[22] (Chicago, 1957).   [23] Ibid., 5.

[24] Ibid., 44.

the rights and the objective incorporation of the responsibility."[25] The intellectual tradition Krieger documents
is one which tended to overlook "that vital theoretical
middle ground between metaphysical and ethical pre-
conceptions and practical consequences."[26] In terms of
realistic novel fictions, it is this middle ground which
produces the specific plasticity of social and moral conflict. But within the German intellectual tradition we
frequently find that reality is either so inherently inimi-
cal to *Geist* as to be not worth a second thought, or that
it is transformed as the palpable, outward realization of
Geist. Either way, the postulation of a significant realm
within which man may come to fulfillment is dependent
upon metaphysical (inward) rather than social (outward) validation. Up to a point, of course, the Bildungsroman partakes of this (questionable) tradition of inwardness. But in my view, the characteristic tension of
Nacheinander and *Nebeneinander* means that the genre
does go some way toward exploring Krieger's "middle
ground."

In many ways, of course, the tradition I have outlined
is a highly unsettling one, even though in the hands of
some of its chief advocates (particularly Goethe and
Schiller) it has a much greater universality and resonance than the above summary has suggested. It is
tempting to dismiss it with a sigh of relief as a typically
German aberration, the terrible historical consequences
of which are universally known. Yet this seems to me a
facile reaction. Clearly, many of the purely theoretical
(that is, philosophical) statements about *Bildung* may be
beyond redemption for the skeptical modern reader,
and it is significant that Krieger is exclusively concerned

[25] Ibid., 69.
[26] Ibid., 301. See also Reinhart Koselleck's discussion of the gulf between moral and politics within bourgeois thinking, *Kritik und Krise*
(Frankfurt, 1976).

with discursively formulated attitudes. But we must recognize that the Bildungsroman is a very different order of statement. It is a fiction in which the concept of *Bildung* is not simply advocated but *embodied* in a life, in experiences described. This very sense of having to try out the theory gives the Bildungsroman a resonance often lacking in the *ex cathedra* theoretical statements about *Bildung*. The fictional result is, as I have tried to suggest in my specific analyses, a novel form that is shot through with irony, with narratively intimated unease. As Lukács implies in his discussion of *Wilhelm Meister's Apprenticeship*,[27] the programmatic undertaking becomes refracted through that wryly "realistic tic" of which Goethe spoke.[28] The novel form makes certain demands within which the concern for *Bildung* must try to operate. For this reason the Bildungsroman is anything but unreflected didacticism; it is, rather, the supreme enactment of that problematic which Krieger and others so precisely perceive.

The Bildungsroman is unthinkable without that state of tension and contradiction between what I have for convenience called the *Nacheinander* of plot and the *Nebeneinander* of human totality and potential. If either pole is obliterated, the lifeblood goes from the genre. The result is either the vague effusions of Novalis's *Heinrich von Ofterdingen* (1802) and the unrelieved discursiveness of Musil's *The Man Without Qualities* (1930-1943) on the one hand, or the smug paean to bourgeois solidity of Freytag's *Debit and Credit* (1855) on the other. The great Bildungsromane inhabit the awkard middle ground between wholeness and constriction, between possibility and actuality. The friction of the genre is the expression of the moral and spiritual uncertainties at the heart of bourgeois society, of an allegiance to practical

---

[27] Lukács, *Goethe und seime, Zeit*, in Lukács, *Werke*, vii (Neuwied and Berlin, 1964), 69-88.
[28] *Hamburger Ausgabe*, viii, 543.

reality *and* to that creative transcendence vouchsafed by the individual's inwardness.[29]

The conflicting norms of this society result from the clash of an individualist economic principle on the one hand, and a moral, indeed religious, conscience that speaks in terms of charity, compassion, and community, on the other. The conflict between the economic law of the jungle and the inward need for a humane collective, between the narrowness of practical living in an increasingly specialized world and the aspirations toward a fuller extension and realization of the human personality—these are, by any standard, central issues in nineteenth-century European fiction. They are not confined to a merely German (that is, parochial) situation. At this level the Bildungsroman is an attempt at mediation between the conflicting pulls of bourgeois society, and it is nowhere more moving and convincing than when that mediation can only be made through uncertain and ironic intimations.

These implications, I would suggest, make this German tradition part of our experience as novel readers. On several occasions throughout this study I have been concerned with Thomas Mann. He is clearly a novelist who enjoys an established international reputation because of (and not in spite of) his thoroughgoing embeddedness in the intellectual, philosophical, and artistic traditions of Germany. Mann's gradual, painful conversion in the 1920s to republicanism, to a creative intellectual engagement with politics, is exemplary in two senses: morally, it is an example that Weimar *Vernunft-republikaner* would have done well to heed; culturally, the difficulty that attended his conversion bespeaks the inescapable resonance of that resolutely "unpolitical"

---

[29] For a telling discussion of these issues see the "Nachwort" to *Theorie und Technik des Romans im 17. und 18. Jahrhundert*, ed. D. Kimpel and C. Wiedemann, II (Tübingen, 1970), 144ff.

tradition for a major European writer.[30] In 1923 Mann commented on the German reverence for *Bildung*:

> The finest characteristic of the typical German, the best-known and also the most flattering to his self-esteem, is his inwardness. It is no accident that it was the Germans who gave to the world the intellectually stimulating and very humane literary form which we call the Bildungsroman. Western Europe has its novel of social criticism, to which the Germans regard this other type as their own special counterpart: it is at the same time an autobiography, a confession. The inwardness, the "Bildung" of a German implies introspectiveness; an individualistic cultural conscience; consideration for the careful tending, the shaping, deepening and perfecting of one's own personality or, in religious terms, for the salvation and justification of one's own life; subjectivism in the things of the mind, therefore, a type of culture that might be called pietistic, given to autobiographical confession and deeply personal, one in which the world of the objective, the political world, is felt to be profane and is thrust aside with indifference, "because," as Luther says, "this external order is of no consequence."[31]

As Bruford has shown in his admirable book,[32] Mann may indeed be the German writer who brings this tradition closest to us—precisely because of his passionate critical debate with it. No one suggested better than he, both in his essays and in his fiction, the resonance and the limitations of that tradition. Just this mixture of

---

[30] For a superb discussion of Mann and his traditions see T. J. Reed, *Thomas Mann: The Uses of Tradition* (Oxford, 1974).

[31] Quoted by Bruford, *German Tradition of Self-Cultivation*, vii.

[32] See n. 31 above.

commitment to and critique of the tradition generated the tentativeness and irony of *The Magic Mountain*. And in this hedging of bets Mann was keeping faith with the Bildungsroman tradition and its deepest problematic. One is tempted to conclude that the Bildungsroman has always been a richer exploration, because more differentiated, of the concept of *Bildung* than are the discursive writings of philosophers and theoreticians. For this reason it is the medium through which a characteristically German preoccupation can speak with greatest urgency to a wider European public.

Excursus:
The Bildungsroman
as a Taxonomic Genre

Throughout this study I have been concerned to explore
the Bildungsroman as a genre which is embedded in the
continuity of one national literature, of one particular
cultural consciousness. I have hoped to demonstrate
that the historical transmission of the tradition is
mediated through the dialectical interaction of novel
theory and novel praxis. It is my contention, then, that
the German Bildungsroman, like any other genre, has
historical specificity. I do not, however, wish to deny
that the genre construct can also be used in a taxonomic
context, that it can serve as a heuristic tool which makes
possible the comparison of a number of texts which
stand in no readily identifiable historical relationship to
one another. There are a number of obvious areas in
which the Bildungsroman model has been and may be
put to such taxonomic use.

With respect to the East German novel, there is of
course a particular historical resonance at work, in the
sense that East German writers see themselves as
legitimate heirs to the tradition of bourgeois humanism,
a tradition which, they argue, has been betrayed by the
capitalist West. One feels this tradition at work in older
fiction, such as Arnold Zweig's *Junge Frau von 1914*
(1931) and *Die Zeit ist reif* (1958), where the center of the
novel is to be found in the individual's attempt to replace his bourgeois (that is, essentially *cultural*) values
with a committed *political* concern for the society around
him. Of more recent novels, Hermann Kant's *Die Aula*
(1966), Erwin Strittmatter's *Ole Bienkopp* (1963), and

Christa Wolf's *Nachdenken über Christa T.* (1968) and *Der geteilte Himmel* (1963) clearly draw on the Bildungsroman genre in their concern for that growing and learning process by which the individual discovers that his self-realization is dependent upon his finding a political community he can affirm. At times these novels in fact feel much less problematic than do their bourgeois forebears: there is not the same sense of the sheer elusiveness (and unrealizability) of the self in all its complexity. But equally, particularly in Wolf, we find a recognition of the psychological difficulty and uncertainty that attends the process by which the individual comes to be and to know himself, a process whose successful outcome cannot be guaranteed by social and political reform.

Another obvious field for the taxonomic application of the Bildungsroman model is the English novel of the nineteenth and early twentieth centuries. Here the Bildungsroman allows for a fruitful comparative exercise. One should note, for example, that Barbara Hardy often invokes the notion of the Bildungsroman, and she is by no means the only critic of the English novel to do so. She sees *The Ambassadors* as a Bildungsroman,[1] a novel in which growth is enacted in terms of sensibility rather than outward actions. *Sons and Lovers*, too, is described as a Bildungsroman,[2] a novel concerned with psychological growth and change rather than with *moral* progress, as in Victorian fiction. Jerome Buckley makes the interesting point in his study of the English Bildungsroman that "in hero and author alike, it is the quickened imagination, moral or aesthetic, that animates and eventually outlives the troubled season of youth."[3] Clearly, there is no shortage of English novels

---

[1] Hardy, *The Appropriate Form: An Essay on the Novel* (London, 1971), 44.

[2] Ibid., 136.

[3] Buckley, *Season of Youth: The Bildungsroman from Dickens to Golding* (Cambridge, Mass., 1974), 282.

concerned with an adolescent's battle for an adequate
extension of the personality, a quest which brings him
into conflict with the constraining factors of parental
wishes and economic and social sanctions. The quickened imagination seeks a realization of itself in a fulfilling marriage, career, etc. Raymond Williams has cogently suggested (and his terms of reference recall the
Bildungsroman) that the dominant motif throughout
the major English novel fictions from Dickens to Lawrence is the quest for a knowable community, for some
objective extension of the individual existence which
will provide a kind of moral and spiritual home.[4]

All these features, of course, have their place in the
German Bildungsroman, except that in the German
novel the quest is defined in epistemological and ontological terms, and not so much with regard to moral,
social, and psychological accommodations. There is,
then, a kind of philosophical radicalism to the German
novelist's undertaking, a radicalism in some ways akin
to what Williams perceives in the later D. H. Lawrence:

> Women in Love . . . is a radical *simplification* of the
> novel, in the interest of a single important empha-
> sis. The concentration on isolated relationships, the
> dropping of other people and of the texture of ordi-
> nary life as irrelevant, had in *The Rainbow* been sim-
> ply the climax of a history. Here it is a whole and
> separate form. . . . I don't want to deny, I would
> prefer to emphasize what Lawrence can then dis-
> cover in radical experience: at the very roots of
> being.[5]

When Lawrence's art approximates to the narrative
situation of the German Bildungsroman, it is the measure of his alienation from that notion of community

---

[4] Williams, *The English Novel from Dickens to Lawrence* (St. Albans, 1974).

[5] Ibid., 145.

which had sustained his earlier fiction. And this perhaps illuminates the decisive difference in emphasis between the German Bildungsroman and its English coun-
terpart: the English novel always maintains a greater
closeness to the actuality of the hero and of the situations with which he is trying to come to terms. There is
not, in other words, the same concern with the definition and validation of human wholeness as mediated
through the person of the protagonist. Both self and
world in the English novel tend to remain clear-cut—
and nowhere more so than in their antagonism. Insofar
as a solution is found, it usually involves a practical accommodation, a *modus vivendi* in which society and the
self have at least some of their rights respected. And if
no solution is found, we at least know that the struggle
we have witnessed is philosophically and morally binding. This has to do with what one critic has perceived as
the lack of philosophical curiosity, the "epistemological
naivety"[6] of literary realism. The German Bildungsroman is rarely guilty of epistemological naivety, though it
may well succumb to (perhaps more damaging)
naiveties. It is noteworthy that we find an attempt to
formulate these differences of cultural outlook in the
one English novel which, in my view, comes closest to
the German Bildungsroman, George Meredith's *The
Adventures of Harry Richmond* (1871). At one point in that
novel, our hero has an interview with a German profes-
sor who, to the complete bafflement of Harry, says:

> You English, fighting your little battles of domestic
> policy, and sneering at us for flying at a higher
> game—you unimpressionable English, who won't
> believe in the existence of aims that don't drop on
> the ground before your eyes, and squat and stare at
> you, you assert that man's labour is completed
> when the poor are kept from crying out. Now my

---

[6] J. P. Stern, *On Realism* (London, 1973), 54.

question is, have you a scheme of life consonant with the spirit of modern philosophy—with the views of intelligent, moral, humane human beings of this period? Or are you one of your robust English brotherhood worthy of a Caligula in his prime, lions in gymnastics—for a time; sheep always in the dominions of the mind; and all of one pattern, all in a rut! Favour me with an outline of your ideas.[7]

Harry's only reply is an awkward silence—and the request for lessons.

I have on several occasions in this study suggested that the German Bildungsroman is a genre which can speak with particular urgency to modern readers. I suspect that for this reason it is a model which can prove helpful for understanding certain kinds of contemporary fiction, by which I mean, of course, not only German fiction. My own feeling is that a novel such as Robert M. Pirsig's *Zen and the Art of Motorcycle Maintenance* (1974) works with precisely the epistemological frame of reference that characterizes the German Bildungsroman. Moreover, I would argue that a number of novels concerned with woman's search for identity, such as Erica Jong's *The Fear of Flying* (1973) and, much more impressively, Doris Lessing's *The Summer before the Dark* (1973), operate with a sense of the elusiveness of the total self which recalls the Bildungsroman. The difficulties attendant upon the heroine's quest for self-knowledge and self-realization are not simply those of outward obstacles—an uncomprehending husband, economic dependence. Indeed, in both of these novels the protagonists are allowed room and time for self-discovery. The obstacles facing them have to do with the terms and parameters of human cognition. It is surely not farfetched to see in *The Summer before the Dark*

[7] Meredith, *The Adventures of Harry Richmond* (London, 1912), 314-15.

aperçus that could well relate to the German Bildungsroman. And, conversely, a knowledge of the
German Bildungsroman can help us better to understand the resonance of that novel:

> We are what we learn.
> It often takes a long and painful time.
> Unfortunately, there was no doubt, either, that a
> lot of time, a lot of pain, went into learning very lit-
> tle. . . .

> Her experiences of the last months—her dis-
> coveries, her self-definition, what she hoped were
> new strengths—were concentrated here: here she
> would walk into her home with her hair undressed,
> with her hair tied straight back for utility; rough
> and streaky, and the widening grey band showing
> like a statement of intent. It was as if the rest of her,
> body, feet, even face, which was aging but amena-
> ble, belonged to everyone else. But her hair—
> no! . . .
> . . . now she was saying no: no, no, no, NO—a
> statement which would be concentrated into hair.
> "I was thinking . . . it seems to me as if little bits
> of me are distributed among my family, Tim's bit,
> Michael's bit, Eileen's piece—and so on. Or rather,
> were distributed. Were. That's over."[8]

[8] Lessing, *The Summer before the Dark* (Harmondsworth, 1975), 8,
230-31.

PRINCETON ESSAYS IN LITERATURE

Adventures in the Deeps of the Mind: The Cuchulain Cycle of W. B. Yeates. By Barton R. Friedman
René Char: The Myth and the Poem. By James R. Lawler
The German Bildungsroman from Wieland to Hesse. By Martin Swales

Index

LIBRARY OF CONGRESS CATALOGING IN
PUBLICATION DATA

Swales, Martin.
  The German Bildungsroman from Wieland to Hesse.

  (Princeton essays in literature)
  Includes index.
    1.   German fiction—History and criticism—
  Addresses, essays, lectures.   I.   Title.
  PT747.E6S9   833'.09   77-85568
  ISBN 0-691-06359-1